Charles Barnard

Knights of today

Love and science

Charles Barnard

Knights of today
Love and science

ISBN/EAN: 9783337281113

Printed in Europe, USA, Canada, Australia, Japan

Cover: Foto ©Andreas Hilbeck / pixelio.de

More available books at **www.hansebooks.com**

OR

LOVE AND SCIENCE

BY

CHARLES BARNARD

NEW YORK

CHARLES SCRIBNER'S SONS

743 AND 745 BROADWAY

1881

PREFATORY NOTE.

----•••----

The accompanying stories, with the exception of "The Sanitary Measure," originally appeared in Scribner's Monthly, Harper's Bazar, *the* Galaxy, *and the* Golden Rule, *and are here collected with the consent of the publishers of those periodicals. The second story is here printed for the first time.*

C. B.

April, 1881.

CONTENTS.

KNIGHTS OF TO-DAY.

AN ELECTRO-MECHANICAL ROMANCE.

CHAPTER I.—THE ENGINE.

SHE was a beauty. From head-light to buffer-casting, from spark-arrester to air-brake coupling, she shone resplendent. A thing of grace and power, she seemed instinct with life as she paused upon her breathless flight. Even while resting quietly upon the track, she trembled with the pulsations of her mighty heart. Small wonder that the passengers waiting upon the platform came down to gaze upon the great express engine, No. 59. She seemed long and slender like a greyhound, and her glistening sides, delicate forefeet, and uplifted head were suggestive of speed and power.

The engineer stepped down from his high throne with his long nickel-plated oiler in hand, and the

fireman clambered over the glistening heap of coal
and swung round the great copper water-pipe that
the magnificent creature might have a drink of
pure spring water. The engineer looked eagerly
up and down the platform as if in search of some
one. Two or three tourists of the usual type and
a stray idler were all to be seen. A group of big
fellows were unloading mail bags, and beyond
them the busy throng down the platform was lost
to view. How lovingly he touched the shining
arms of his great pet with the smooth clear oil,
golden and limpid. Here her great cylinder,
seventeen inches wide, and with a stroke of twenty-
four, safely rested behind the sturdy buttress that
held her forefoot so daintily thrust out in front.
The head-light gleamed in all the sparkle of plate-
glass, and her shapely rods fairly glowed in polished
beauty. On one side lay her boiler-feed pump, a
finished bit of mechanism, and on the other was
hung a steam-injector for forcing water into the
boiler without the aid of the pump. How perfect
everything! Even the driving-wheels were works
of art. From balanced throttle-valves to air-brake
she had every device that American skill had produced, or that such an engine could demand, and
her thirty-five tons of chained-up energy seemed
the perfect expression of the highest mechanic art.

With a loud roar her safety-valve yielded to her
pent-up vitality and filled all the air with clouds

of steam. The engineer gazed proudly upon his noble steed, and then looked anxiously down the platform to see if any came whose presence would be welcome.

The fireman swung back the great copper pipe, and the idlers suddenly withdrew. The last trunk was thrown in, and the engineer climbed slowly up into his house. He looked anxiously about the long platform. It was nearly clear, and he could see the gold band on the conductor's hat glistening in the sun.

Where can she linger? Why does she not come? 59 is here, and still she comes not. The gold-banded cap is lifted in the air. With one hand on the throttle-valve, the engineer glances down the long empty platform. The bell rings; there is a hissing sound beneath the giant's feet; the house trembles slightly; the water-tank seems to move backward; the roar of the safety-valve suddenly stops; the fury of the great iron monster vents itself in short deep gasps; clouds of smoke pour down on everything. They almost hide the platform from view.

Ah! A dress fluttering in the door-way. Some one appears abruptly upon the platform. With both hands on the throttle-valve, the engineer leans out the window. A handkerchief is quickly flirted in the air. He nods, smiles, and then turns grimly away, and stares out ahead with a fixed look as if the world had suddenly grown very dark, and life was an iron road with dangers everywhere. The fireman shovels coal into the fiery cavern at the engineer's feet, and then stirs up the glowing mass till it roars and flames with fury. The steam-gauge trembles at 120°, and quickly rises to 125°. The vast engine trembles and throbs as it leaps forward. The landscape—woods, houses and fields seem to take wings in a wild, Titanic waltz. The engineer gazes ahead with tight-set lips, but his heart can outrun his locomotive, and lingers behind at the deserted way-station.

CHAPTER II.—THE TELEGRAPH OPERATOR.

WITH that perversity for which railroads are famous, the line did not enter the town, but passed along its outermost edge, among the farms and woodlands. This affected the life of the place curiously. At one hour the station was animated and thronged with people; at another it was dull, quiet and deserted by all save the station-master and his daughter. She it was who guarded the little telegraph office, received and sent the telegrams of the town, and did anything else that pertained to her position. She had a little box of a place portioned off in one corner of the ladies' waiting-room, where there was a sunny window that looked far up the line, and a little opening where she received the messages. She viewed life through this scant outlook, and thought it very queer. Were people always in a state of excitement? Did everybody have trouble in the family that demanded such breathless, heart-rending messages? Was it in every life to have these awful, sudden things happen? Life from her point of view was more tragic than joyful, and she sometimes thought it a relief to receive a prosy order to "tell Jones bring back boots and have mower mended." Sometimes between the trains the station was quite deserted, and were it not for the ticking of the clock, and the incessant rattle of the fretful machine on her desk, it would be as still as a church on Monday. At first she amused herself by listening to the strange language of the wires, and she even made the acquaintance of the other operators. With one exception they all failed to interest her. They were a frivolous set, and their chatter seemed as empty as the rattle of a brass sounder. One girl she knew must be a lady. Her style of touch, and the general manner of her work, showed that plainly, and between the two a friendship sprang up, though they lived a hundred miles apart, and had never met. Finally, she took wisely to reading books, and the sounder chattered in vain, except on business.

Then there was John. She saw him for one

hurried moment every day, and the thinking of it filled many a weary hour. He was the engineer of the express, and stopped at the station every afternoon at five and just before daylight every morning. She met him at the water-tank by day, and by night she awoke to hear his train thunder through the valley. She heard it whistle as it passed the grade crossing, a mile up the line, and as it pulled up at the station. If the night was calm, she heard the faint rumble as it flew over the resounding iron bridge at the river. Then she slept again. He would soon reach the city, and on the morrow she would see him again.

The happy morrow always found her at her post, busy and cheerful as the long day crept away, and the time drew near for his train. Oh! if her window only looked out the other way, that she might see No. 59 come round the curve in the woods! The station was always full at that hour, and messages were sure to come in just as she wanted to close her little office and go out to the water-tank, where John waited, oiler in hand, to see her. Strange, that he should always be oiling up just there.

This time, she waited with calm face and beating heart to see if any stupid passenger had forgotten anything, that he must telegraph home. Fortunately, none came, and as the engine rolled past her window she hastily put on her pretty hat and ample cloak and went out on the platform. A few quick steps, and she was beside the noble 59.

The fireman smiled a grimy smile, and, while he swung the water-pipe over the tender, he gave a lively whistle. The engineer tipped up his oiler with a sudden jerk, as if the piston-rod had quite enough, and then climbed hastily into the cab. There she sat on the fireman's perch, radiant, blushing, and winsome.

" She's a beauty—perfectly lovely, and a West-inghouse, too! I tried to see you yesterday, and aren't you very proud of her ? "

John thought he was rather proud of 59. She was perfect. Ran her one hundred and fifty miles yesterday for the first time. The little electrician was charmed. To think that John should be appointed master over the Company's new express engine. Dear fellow, he had run that old 13, till she was ready to rattle to pieces. And now, what a mag-nificent machine he had beneath him !

" And everything is so bright and handsome. I know you're proud of her."

John thought he was also proud of somebody else. Then they smiled, and the fireman whistled softly as he pushed back the water-spout. How brief the precious moments !

John pulled out a little blank-book and began hastily to tell about the new prize the Directors had offered to the engineer who should travel five thousand miles with the least expenditure of coal and oil. It would take about twenty-seven days to decide the matter, and then the books would be all handed in, and the records examined, and the prize awarded.

"And if we could get it!"

"It would come in very convenient for——"

She blushed a rosy blush, and clasping his arm, she laughed softly, and said :

"My dear, you must win it. We shall want it for—our——"

"Lively, now ! Here comes the Conduc."

What a friendly fireman ! How sharp he watched for the lovers ! The girl prepared to spring down from the engine when the gold-banded cap of the conductor came in sight.

"Run up to the siding, Mills, and bring down that extra car."

"Aye, aye, sir. Cast off the couplings, Dick." Then, in a whisper : "Wait a bit, Kate. Ride up to the siding with us."

The girl needed no invitation.

"Oh, I intended to. Here, let me tend the bell."

"Good ! Do. Dick must tend the couplings."

With a hiss and a jar the monster started forward, while the girl sat on the fireman's high seat with her hand on the bell-rope and one little foot steadied against the boiler. Suddenly, John turned the valve for the air-brake and reversed his lever, and the monster stopped. A deafening blast from the whistle.

"Where is that signal man? Why don't he show his flag?"

Again the whistle roared in short, quick blasts.

"Oh! Why didn't I think of it before?"

"Think of what?"

"That whistle. You could use it to call me."

"When?"

"Why, you see, I never exactly know when you are coming. I cannot tell your whistle from any other, and so, I sometimes miss seeing you."

"I—have—noticed—that——" said John, pulling at the throttle-valve. "But, what can I do? If I gave two whistles or three, they would think it meant some signal, and it would make trouble."

"Yes, but if you did this, I should know you were coming, and nobody would think anything of it."

So saying, she stood up, leaned over the boiler, and grasping the iron rod that moved the whistle, made it speak in long and short blasts, that may be represented as follows:

"——— — ——— — —— —— —"

"I see. Like a sounder. Morse's alphabet. But what does it spell?"

"K ———.—— A -.—— T —— E -"

1*

" Oh ! Let me learn that by heart."

" You must, John. And will it not be amusing to hear the folks talk ? What on earth can that engineer be roaring about with his ' ⎯⎯ ⎯ ⎯⎯ ⎯ ⎯⎯ ⎯⎯ ⎯ ' "

The signal-man looked indignant as 59 rolled past him. What was the good of such a din on the whistle ! Was the man crazy !

"You must write it down, Kate. It won't do to practise now. See how the people stare on—the —platform."

The sentence was broken up by John's efforts over the reversing bar, and the deep-toned gasps of the engine drowned further conversation. The monster backed into the siding, where Dick stood ready to couple on the extra car. Then he climbed up into the cab, and the lovers were silenced. The engine, with the three, rolled out upon the main line, stopped, and then backed up to the train. Kate, with a pencil wrote some marks on the edge of the window-frame, and with a bright smile she shook hands with the burly engineer, nodded to the fireman, and then sprang lightly to the ground.

The safety-valve burst out with a deafening roar. The smoke belched forth in clouds, and while fairy rings of steam shot into the air, the train moved slowly away.

Presently, the girl stood alone upon the deserted

platform, with the ruddy glow of the setting sun gilding her bright face.

The roar of the train melted away on the air. Still, she stood listening intently. She would wait till she heard him whistle at the next crossing. Then, like a mellow horn softened by the distance, came this strange rhythmic song :

A smile and a blush lit up her winsome face.

How quickly love can learn !

That night, the waning moon sank cold and white in the purple west, while the morning star came out to see the sleeping world. Kate awoke suddenly and listened. Was that the roar of his train ?

" How soft and sweet the notes so far away ! There ! He has crossed the bridge. Dear John !"

Then she slept again.

CHAPTER III.—THE OTHER OPERATOR.

THE last local train to the city left the station. The gray old station-master put out the lamps on the platform, rolled the baggage-trucks into the freight-house, and, having made the tour of the switches to see that all was clear for the main-line night mail, he returned to his little ticket den.

His daughter still sat reading like a demure puss in her little corner. The old man remarked that it was ten o'clock, and time to go home.

"Leave the key, father; I'll lock up and return home as soon as I have finished this chapter."

The old fellow silently laid a bunch of keys on her desk and went his way. The moment he departed she finished her chapter in a flash, and laying the book down, began to operate her telegraphic apparatus.

$$\text{—— —— —— —— —— —— —— ——.}$$

No reply. Middleboro had evidently gone to bed, and that office was closed.

$$\cdot \text{—— ——} \cdot \text{—— —— —— ——.}$$

No response. Dawson City refused to reply. Good. Now, if the operator at the junction failed to reply, she and Mary would have the line to themselves with none to overhear.

$$\text{— —— — —— — —— — ——.}$$

Allston Junction paid no heed. Good. Now for :

$$\text{—— —— — —— — —— —— ——.}$$

Mary replied instantly, and at once the two girl-friends were in close conversation with one hundred miles of land and water between them. The conversation was by sound in a series of long and short notes—nervous and staccato for the bright one in the little station; smooth, legato and placid for the city girl.

Translated, it ran as follows:

Kate—" I taught him my name in Morse's alphabet, and he sounds it on his whistle as he comes up to the station; but I am in daily terror lest some impertinent operator should hear it, and, catching its meaning, tell of it."

The other operator was all sympathy, and replied:

" I see the danger. At the same time, my dear, I think the idea is worthy of your bright self. It is perfectly jolly. Think of hearing one's name for miles over the country on a steam-whistle. I never heard of anything so romantic in my life."

Kate—" And when he passes in the night he sounds my name all through the valley, and I can hear it for miles. How people would laugh if they knew what it meant."

Mary—" They would, I'm sure, and it would be very unpleasant to be found out. Why don't you fix up some kind of open circuit and let him telegraph to you from the line as he approaches your station ? "

Kate—" My love, your idea is divine. If I only had a wire."

Mary—" It would take two wires, you know, and a small battery. At the same time, it would not cost much, and would be perfectly safe."

Kate—" Would not some one find it out and be ringing the bell out of mischief ? "

Mary—" No. You could hide the connections in the bushes or trees by the road, and his engine could touch it as it passed."

Kate—" Yes, but wouldn't every engine touch it ? "

Mary—" Then you could fix it so that a stick, or something secured to the engine, would brush it as it passed. No other engine would be provided with the stick, and they would all pass in silence."

The idea was almost too brilliant for contemplation, and the two friends, one in her deserted and lonely station in the far country, and the other in the fifth story of a city block, held close converse over it for an hour or more, and then they bid each other good-night, and the wires were at rest for a time.

About five one afternoon shortly after, Kate sat in her office waiting for 59 to sound its Titanic love-signal. Presently it came in loud-mouthed notes :

" —— – —— – —— —— – "

She closed her little office hastily, and went out on the platform. As she opened the door, two young men laughed immoderately, and one said

" Kate ! Who's Kate ? "

Found out ! She hastily turned away to hide the blush that mounted to her temples and walked rapidly up the platform to the water-tank.

59 rolled up to the spot, and the lovers met.
With one hand on the iron front of his great engine, she stood waiting for him, and at once began to talk rapidly.

" It will never do, John ! They have found it all
out."

" Oh ! I was afraid they would. Now, what are
we to do ? If I could only telegraph you from the
station below."

" It wouldn't do. It is too far away. Besides,
it would be costly, and somebody would suspect."

" Conduc ! " shouted the fireman, as he swung
back the great water-pipe.

" Good-by, dear ! I'm sorry we must give it
up."

" So am I. And, John, come and spend next
Sunday with us."

" Yes, I will. Good-by, Good-by."

59 hissed out her indignation in clouds of steam
from her cylinders, and moved slowly forward.
Then Kate stood alone again on the platform.
The sun sank in angry clouds, and the wind sighed
in the telegraph wires with a low moaning sound,
fitful, sad and dreary.

The next morning the express tore savagely
through the driving rain, and thundered over the
iron bridge till it roared again. The whistle
screamed, but love no longer charmed its iron
voice.

The electrician listened in silence, and then, after a tear or two, slept again.

CHAPTER IV.—LOVE AND LIGHTNING.

IT was a lovely autumnal afternoon, and the lovers went out to walk in the glorious weather.

To escape observing eyes, they wandered down the railroad track toward the woods, where the line made a great curve to avoid a bend in the river.

After a while they reached a shady dell in the woods, and, taking down a bar in the fence, they entered its depths. Just here the various telegraph wires hung in long festoons from their poles. With a sudden cry of delight, she seized his arm and cried :

" Look, John. Just the thing. An abandoned wire."

" Well ; what of it ? "

" My dear, can't we use it ? Come, let us follow it and see where it goes. Perhaps we may make it useful."

John failed to see how that might be. Kate was all eagerness to follow the wire, and returned to the track, and began to trace the wire up and down the line as far as it was visible. John replaced the fence rail and joined her. Then she began to talk in that rapid manner that was so becoming to her. He was fairly dazzled by the brilliancy and audacity of her ideas. They both walked on the sleepers toward the bridge over the river. The wire was still continuous, but after walking about half a mile, they found it was broken, and apparently abandoned. Then she laid down her plan. This wire had been put up by a certain company some years since, but as the company had failed, the wire had been abandoned, and here for perhaps a mile it was still hanging on its insulators. At the bridge it came to a sudden end.

"Now, if we can manage to rig up another wire .from here to our station we can make an open circuit, and as you pass this point you can join it and —ring a bell in my office!"

The two sat down on the iron bridge and fairly laughed at the splendor of the idea. Suddenly she looked very grave.

"The expense!"

"Ah! yes. Well, I'm willing to pay something for the advantage of seeing you every day. It's worth——"

"How much?"

"About $5,000,000."

"John!"

Two days after, a package came by express from the city, and Kate stowed it away in her telegraphic den till the evening. Then, when the day had passed, and she had some leisure, she carefully opened it and found a neat little wooden box with a small brass gong or bell attached to the bottom. A slender hammer hung beside it, and there were places for securing the connecting wires, an electric bell and 3,000 feet of insulated wire and a bill for the same. Eleven dollars.

" Not half so bad as I expected. As for the battery, I fancy I can make one myself. A pickle-jar, some zinc and copper and a little acid will answer, and John can arrange the rest. Fortunately I selected insulated wire, as we shall have to carry our line through the woods to cut off that bend in the road."

Thus talking and planning to herself, she examined her purchase, and then carefully placing the bell and the wire in a closet under her desk, she closed up the station and went demurely home, conscious of the innocence of all her dark plottings.

The third day after seemed like the Sabbath, and was not. It was Thanksgiving Day, and all the very good people went soberly to church. The good people like Kate and her lover did nothing of the kind. John Mills, engineer, did not ride on No. 59 that day. He had a holiday, and came to see Kate quite early in the morning. She proposed a walk in the woods, as the day was fine.

" Did you bring the boots ? "

" I did, my love, spikes and all. I tried 'em on an apple-tree, and I found I could walk up the stem as nicely as a fly on the ceiling."

" That is good ; for, on the whole, I think we must shorten the line, and cut off that great bend in the road."

" And save battery power? "

" Yes. My pickle-jar battery works well, but I find that it is not particularly powerful. It rings the bell furiously when I close the circuit, but the circuit is not two yards long. What it will do when the line is up, remains to be seen."

" Where did you place the bell ? "

" Oh, I hung it up in the cupboard under my desk. I can hear it and no one will be likely to look for it there. But that is not the great difficulty. How are we to hide the wires that enter the station ? "

" I wouldn't try. Let them stand in plain sight. Not a soul will ever notice them among the crowd of wires that pass the station."

By this time the two had reached the railroad station, and, opening her little office, they both went in. Presently they reappeared, each with a brown paper parcel, and, with the utmost gravity, walked away down the line toward the woods.

In a few moments they were lost to view beyond a curve in the road, and they turned off toward the bank and sat down on a large, flat stone.

" The boots, Kate."

She opened the bundle she had in her hand, and displayed a pair of iron stirrups having an iron rod on one side, and a sharp steel point on the bottom. There were also leather straps and buckles, and John, laying aside his burden, proceeded to strap them to his feet. When ready, the iron rods or bars reached nearly to the knee, and the steel points were just below the instep. Kate meanwhile took a pair of stout shears from her pocket and began to open the other bundle. It contained a large roll of insulated copper wire, some tacks, and a hammer.

Then they started down the track, with sharp eyes on the abandoned wire hanging in long festoons from its insulators. All right so far. Ah! a break; they must repair it. Like a nimble cat John mounted the pole, and Kate unrolled the wire as he took it up. In a moment or two he had it secured to the old wire. Then up the next pole, and while Kate pulled it tight he secured it, and the line was reunited.

Then on and on they walked, watching the wire, and still finding it whole. At last they reached the great iron bridge, and anxiously scanned the dozen or more wires, to see if their particular thread was still continuous.

"We must cross the river, John. The line seems to be whole, and we can take our new line through the woods on the other shore till we reach the town bridge."

It was a relief to leave the dizzy open sleepers of the bridge and stand once more on firm ground.

"This must be the limit of our circuit. I wish it was larger, for it will not give me more than three minutes' time. Now, if you'll break the line on that pole, John."

There was a sound of falling glass, and then the new insulated line was secured to the old line ; the broken end fell to the ground and was abandoned. For half an hour or more the two were busy over their work, and then it was finished. It was a queer-looking affair, and no one would ever guess where it was or what it was designed to do. A slender maple-tree beside the track had a bit of bare copper wire (insulated at the ends), hung upright, in its branches. Near by stood a large oak-tree, also having a few feet of wire secured horizontally to its branches. From the slender maple a wire ran to the old telegraph line. From the old oak our young people quickly ran a new line through the woods by simply tacking it up out of sight in the trees.

Then they came to the wooden bridge where the town road crossed the stream. It took but a few moments to tack the insulated wire to the under side of one of the string-pieces well out of sight, and then they struck off into the deep woods again.

Three hours later they struck the railroad, and found the old wire some distance beyond the sta-

tion up the line.   Again the two-legged cat ran up
the pole, and there was a sound of breaking glass.
The old wire fell down among the bushes, and the
new one was joined to the piece still on the line.
A short time after, two young people with rather
light bundles and very light hearts gravely walked
into the station and then soberly went to their dinner.   That night two mysterious figures flitted
about the platform of the deserted station.   One
like a cat ran up the dusky poles, and the other
unrolled a bit of copper wire.   There was a sound
of boring, and two minute wires were pushed
through a hole in the window frame.   The great
scientific enterprise was finished.

CHAPTER V.—ALMOST TELESCOPED.

IT was very singular how absent-minded and in-
attentive the operator was that day.   She sent that
order for flowers to the butcher, and Mrs. Robin-
son's message about the baby's croup went to old
Mr. Stimmins, the bachelor lodger at the gambrel-
roofed house.

No wonder she was disturbed.   Would the new
line work?   Would her pickle-jar battery be strong
enough for such a great circuit?   Would John be
able to close it?   The people began to assemble
for the train.   The clock pointed to the hour for
its arrival.

"He cometh not," she said. Then she began to be a little fearful. The people all left the waiting-room and went out on the platform, and the place was deserted and silent. She listened intently. There was nothing, save the murmur of the voices outside, and the irritating tick of the clock.

Suddenly, with startling distinctness, the bell rang clear and loud in the echoing room. With a cry of delight she put on her dainty hat and ran in haste out upon the platform. The idle people stared at her flushed and rosy face, and she turned away and walked toward the water-tank. Not a thing in sight? What did it mean?

Ah! The whistle broke loud and clear on the cool, crisp air, and 59 appeared round the curve in the woods. The splendid monster slid swiftly up to her feet and paused.

"Perfect, John! Perfect! It works to a charm."

With a spring she reached the cab and sat down on the fireman's seat.

"Blessed if I could tell what he was going to do," said Dick. "He told me about it. Awful bright idea! You see, he laid the poker on the tender brake there, and it hit the tree slam, and I saw the wires touch. It was just prime!"

. The happy moments sped, and 59 groaned and slowly departed, while Kate stood on the platform, her face wreathed in smiles and white steam.

So the lovers met each day, and none knew how

she was made aware of his approach with such ab-
solute certainty.   Science applied to love, or
rather love applied to science, can move the
world.

Two whole weeks passed, and then there suddenly arrived at the station, late one evening, a
special with the directors' car attached.   The honorable directors were hungry—they always are—
and would pause on their journey and take a cup
of tea and a bit of supper.   The honorables and
their wives and children filled the station, and the
place put on quite a gala aspect.   As for Kate, she
demurely sat in her den, book in hand, and over
its unread pages admired the gay party in the
brightly lighted waiting-room.

Suddenly, with furious rattle her electric bell
sprang into noisy life.   Every spark of color left
her face, and her book fell with a dusty slam to the
floor.   What was it?   What did it mean?   Who
rang it?

With affrighted face she burst from her office
and brushed through the astonished people and
out upon the snow-covered platform.   There stood
the directors' train upon the track of the on-com-
ing engine.

"The conductor!   Where is he?   Oh!   sir!
Start!   Start!   Get to the siding!   The express!
The express is coming!"

With a cry she snatched a lantern from a brakeman's hand, and in a flash was gone. They saw her light pitching and dancing through the darkness, and they were lost in wonder and amazement. The girl is crazy! No train is due now! There can be no danger. She must be ——

Ah! that horrible whistle. Such a wild shriek on a winter's night! The men sprang to the train, and the women and children fled in frantic terror in every direction.

"Run for your lives," screamed the conductor. "There's a smash-up coming!"

A short, sharp scream from the whistle. The head-light gleamed on the snow-covered track, and there was a mad rush of sliding wheels and the gigantic engine roared like a demon. The great 59 slowly drew near and stopped in the woods. A hundred heads looked out, and a stalwart figure leaped down from the engine and ran on into the bright glow of the head-light.

"Kate!"

"Oh! John, I ——"

She fell into his arms senseless and white, and the lantern dropped from her nerveless hand.

They took her up tenderly and bore her into the station-house and laid her upon the sofa in the "ladies' room." With hushed voices they gathered round to offer aid and comfort. Who was she? How did she save the train? How did she know of its approach?

2

"She is my daughter," said the old station-master. "She tends the telegraph."

The President of the Railroad, in his gold-bowed spectacles, drew near. One grand lady in silk and satin pillowed Kate's head on her breast. They all gathered near to see if she revived. She opened her eyes and gazed about dreamily, as if in search of something.

"Do you wish anything, my dear?" said the President, taking her hand.

"Some water, if you please, sir; and I want— I want——"

They handed her some wine in a silver goblet. She sipped a little, and then looked among the strange faces as if in search of some one.

"Are you looking for any one, Miss?"

"Yes—no—it is no matter. Thank you, ma'am, I feel better. I sprained my foot on the sleepers when I ran down the track. It is not severe, and I'll sit up."

They were greatly pleased to see her recover, and a quiet buzz of conversation filled the room. How did she know it? How could she tell the special was chasing us? Good Heavens! if she had not known it, what an awful loss of life there would have been; it was very careless in the superintendent to follow our train in such a reckless manner.

"You feel better, my dear," said the President.

" Yes, sir, thank you. I'm sure I'm thankful. I knew John—I mean the engine was coming."

" You cannot be more grateful than we are to you for averting such a disastrous collision."

" I'm sure, I am pleased, sir. I never thought the telegraph——"

She paused abruptly.

" What telegraph ? "

" I'd rather not tell, sir."

" But you will tell us how you knew the engine was coming ? "

" Must you know ? "

" We ought to know in order to reward you properly."

She put up her hand in a gesture of refusal, and was silent. The President and directors consulted together, and two of them came to her and briefly said that they would be glad to know how she had been made aware of the approaching danger.

" Well, sir, if John is willing, I will tell you all. "

John Mills, engineer, was called, and he came in, cap in hand, and the entire company gathered round in the greatest eagerness.

Without the slightest affectation, she put her hand on John's grimy arm, and said :

" Shall I tell them, John ? They wish to know about it. It saved their lives, they say."

"And mine, too," said John, reverently. "You had best tell them, or let me."

She sat down again, and then and there John explained how the open circuit line had been built, how it was used, and frankly told why it had been erected.

Never did story create profounder sensation. The gentlemen shook hands with him, and the President actually kissed her for the Company. A real Corporation kiss, loud and hearty. The ladies fell upon her neck, and actually cried over the splendid girl. Even the children pulled her dress, and put their arms about her neck, and kissed away the happy tears that covered her cheeks.

Poor child! She was covered with confusion, and knew not what to say or do, and looked imploringly to John. He drew near, and proudly took her hand in his, and she brushed away the tears and smiled.

The gentlemen suddenly seemed to have found something vastly interesting to talk about, for they gathered in a knot in the corner of the room. Presently the President said aloud:

"Gentlemen and Directors, you must pardon me, and I trust the ladies will do the same, if I call you to order for a brief matter of business."

There was a sudden hush, and the room, now packed to suffocation, was painfully quiet.

" The Secretary will please take minutes of this meeting."

The Secretary sat down at Kate's desk, and then there was a little pause.

" Mr. President ! "

Every eye was turned to a corner where a gray-haired gentleman had mounted a chair.

" Mr. President."

" Mr. Graves, director for the State, gentlemen."

" I beg leave, sir, to offer a resolution."

Then he began to read from a slip of paper.

" Whereas, John Mills, engineer of engine Number 59, of this railway line, erected a private telegraph ; and, whereas he, with the assistance of the telegraph operator of this station (I leave a. blank for her name), used the said line without the consent of this Company, and for other than railway business :

" It is resolved that he be suspended permanently from his position as engineer, and that the said operator be requested to resign——"

A murmur of disapprobation filled the room, but the President commanded silence, and the State Director went on.

"——resign her place.

" It is further resolved, and is hereby ordered, that the said John Mills be and is appointed chief engineer of the new repair shops at Slawson."

A tremendous cheer broke from the assembled

company, and the resolution was passed with a shout of assent.

How it all ended they never knew. It seemed like a dream, and they could not believe it true till they stood alone in the winter's night on the track beside that glorious 59. The few cars the engine had brought up had been joined to the train, and 59 had been rolled out on the siding. With many hand-shakings for John, and hearty kisses for Kate, and a round of parting cheers for the two, the train had sped away. The idlers had dispersed, and none lingered about the abandoned station save the lovers. 59 would stay that night on the siding, and they had walked up the track to bid it a long farewell.

For a few moments they stood in the glow of the great lamp, and then he quietly put it out, and left the giant to breathe away its fiery life in gentle clouds of white steam. As for the lovers, they had no need of its light. The winter's stars shone upon them, and the calm cold night seemed a paradise below.

A SANITARY MEASURE.

" THINGS cannot go on in this way much longer. What do you propose to do about it ? "

" The problem is not peculiar.   On one side the necessity of doing something for the sanitary well-being of the boys and girls, on the other, the state of the family Treasury Department."

Thus said Mrs. Deliverance Scantacre, to her husband Peregrine Scantacre, the father of her large and interesting family of children, and thus it was he had replied.   Upon which she added :

" Bring your science to bear on the subject, Professor.   You are a true New Englander and well able to invent a way out of any difficulty.   What is the use of being a Professor of Applied Physics if you can't keep your children in good health ? "

" My dear, you always trip on technical subjects.   The sun is a star of variable magnitude, and just now it is on one of its most disagreeable variations—the weather is simply terrible."

" And before July we may be all down in our beds.   Poor Patience is beginning to droop, and

Silvia and Deliverance are quite listless. Melancthon and little Perri were both feverish last night,
I expect every day all the others will be down with
the heat."

The Professor suggested a long visit to the sea-
side boarding-house on the Sound, where they had
spent the last summer. It would never do. Three
adults, and nine children in one small farm house.
She could not go through such an experience
again. A quiet farm house among the Berkshire
Hills. She was sure mountain-air was not the
thing needed. The children must have sea-air.
Stay in New York and go to Manhattan Beach once
or twice a week. She would not even consider it.
Every trip last summer had cost one dollar and ten
cents for each, or fourteen dollars and thirty cents
for five hours by the sea, including a lunch that
couldn't in courtesy be called a dinner.

Professor Scantacre took up his duties at the
University that morning with a sad heart. The
problem before the house was a simple, perhaps a
dull and prosy one, yet one that many a city family has to face and solve as best it may. How escape the heat of the town without enduring untold
discomforts in a wretched boarding-house, or paying a preposterous price for only moderate comfort in a hotel. To the Professor, loving his home
and family life, the bare idea of boarding seemed
dismal and forlorn to the last degree. He had

lived under his own roof in a simple and quiet way for twenty years. All his thoughts and habits were tuned to domestic life. The long vacation had always been a trial, and once more the annual problem had come up—Where shall·they go, how spend the summer ? How live by the sea and yet be at home ? They had tried everything, fisherman's house, farm house, hotels, camping out, and the short-trip plan. Staying in town was a hollow mockery, boarding was to be avoided as one would the malaria and camping out, while it was wonderfully private and home-like, had its drawbacks, particularly when the wind blew the tent down in the middle of a rainy night, and a colony of ants established themselves in the pantry.

" A family of eleven, and a fixed and limited income presents a problem in social statics more easy to describe than to solve. The connection between the Solar spots and my income needs readjustment. If I could only pick up the house and set it on piles in the sea after the manner of the Lake Dwellers——"

The Professor never finished his remark, for active mind leaped nimbly to a new train of thought. The school-room was hot and dusty, and the Professor's charming lecture on the Coefficient of Expansion seemed lacking in those poetical and scientific features that at times lighted up this absorbing topic. The pupils marvelled as much as was desirable considering the state of the thermometer, and excused everything. It was too warm to be particular about anything—save the long vacation.

Late that afternoon the Professor came home to dinner, and gravely asked his wife how many beds there were in the house.

"There's Aunt Jane's and Patience's, the double cottage in Deliverance's and Silvia's room; there's one each for Melancthon and Peregrine, and Elijah, Thomas, and William have one between them, and there's the baby's crib and the spare bed in the third floor back, and ours and two in the girl's room. Twelve beds and fourteen people. Quite a sizable family, Professor."

"Quite so, my dear. Now, could you manage to get on with only nine beds and one girl?"

Mrs. Deliverance said she could if she must.

"I intend to keep house by the sea, or rather on the sea, and I was thinking how the rooms could be arranged."

The Professor was one of those wise men who lay all their hopes and plans before their entire household. It was a republican family, and so, when the great dining-room table had been cleared, they met, as a committee of the whole, on the summer vacation. Father Scantacre always presided at these meetings, while Mother Deliverance held the veto power. That's the way they put it, though Mrs. Professor had never been known to veto anything that contributed to her children's happiness.

The Professor laid his plans before the house. Brother-in-law Snow, of Snow, Scauldfield & Butterworth, lumber dealers, Hunter's Point, owned an old scow or timber float. It was now hauled up at the yard. The Professor had been over that afternoon to see it. It leaked slightly, but a few dollars would mend that, and a coat of paint would make it look quite respectable. We will put a one-story house on the boat, divide it into rooms, move the furniture in and keep house on board till the Fall."

A shout of joy from the boys, laughter from the girls, and a smile from Aunt Jane greeted this remarkable proposal. Mrs. Deliverance did not even smile.

" I'm sure, Professor, we can never think of living at that wretched Hunter's Point."

" No, my dear, we will anchor the noble craft behind the beach at Sandy Hook, and live aboard in all the glorious freedom of the prehistoric man."

As the full splendor of the idea dawned upon them, they broke out into a hundred suggestions and remarks of a pleasing character.

They could fish from the parlor window, see the ships go by the front door, spend the summer on

the sea, and yet be at home, and be gently rocked
on the cradle of the deep in the most entrancing
manner.

" And I dare say I shall have every one of you
down with sea-sickness."

" The old float is twenty feet wide," said the
Professor. " It will sit any ordinary waves in the
bay like a rock ; besides, the ventilation will be
perfect, and there will be no ill-smelling machinery
on board. In fact it will be really quite a sanitary
measure."

Just then a visitor to see Patience was announced.
She went to the parlor to receive her guest, while
the family considered the sanitary measure. The
more they examined it the more brilliant it seemed,
and it was generally accepted that if it did not cost
too much it must be done.

Patience Scantacre was one of those loving and
lovable girls brought up in an atmosphere of domestic affection and liberal culture, who do so much
to make the American name respected. Her father's position in society was excellent. She had
inherited a love of study and the chance to win the
best culture the land affords. She had received at
her father's hands the same scientific education
given to his pupils, and while not a classical scholar
she was something far better—a mistress of physics, a practical engineer and theoretical machinist.
Her position was like that of many another Amer-

ican girl. She was in the best society, and yet her father was comparatively a poor man.

Society had received her on account of her beauty and winsome manners, and it forgave her rather formidable education. It is a rule of Society that no one must intrude his learning upon the placid and shallow stream of thought in which it lives. To be cultivated in a broad sense is to be "peculiar." To be "peculiar" is almost as good as being morally bad. Patience knew this, and in the presence of Society tuned herself to Society's diapason. In this she had a reason, perhaps not wholly wise, yet natural and womanly. She loved art, luxury, handsome drawing-rooms and fine dresses. These things she found in Society, and she forgave the vapid and shallow life for the sake of its pleasures.

In Society she had met many young men, chiefly nobodies, and among them had come Clarence Trefoil. He had seemed at first much like the rest, a man of some means, of only superficial education, a good heart, and empty because idle, head. He had shown a sincere admiration for Patience Scantacre, and she in turn had first laughed at him, then endured him, and, at last, had grown interested in him very much as she might be in some silent piece of machinery of which she understood the several parts, but could not guess its aim or actual outcome when in operation.

His object in calling this evening was to bid her good-by for the summer, the gay season in town being now at an end. He was off on a cruise in his steam-yacht, "the Sylphide," on the morrow. Patience was delighted to hear of his pleasant prospects for the summer.

"I, too, love the sea, and it is just possible we may take a trip in father's new boat."

"Has your father a yacht? What's its name? Of course he's in some yacht club."

"Oh, no. It's not a yacht. It's only a sanitary measure. It's not so much as launched yet, much less named."

The young man was puzzled for a moment. This girl was far more clever than he, and at times he could not, at once, understand her. All he could say was that he was glad she was going on the water in a boat of some kind.

"I admire the sea. It seems to build a fellow up and make him feel as if he was a man and a master. I sometimes think that if I lost my money I would be a sea captain."

The subject seemed to wake him from the vacant and affected "tone" which Society had prescribed as the correct thing in a young man, and for the moment Patience thought he really seemed manly and intelligent. He tried to win from her the name of her father's boat and its probable destination, but she would tell nothing more, and at last he went away, and they parted with mutual good wishes for the summer and a hope that perhaps they might meet upon the water.

" It may be the sea will make a man of him. I dare say a good lively storm and real danger would shake off the silly crust he thinks Society bids him wear. And then I wonder what would be found beneath—perhaps a man."

Thus it was she spoke to herself as she closed the door upon him and returned to the family council.

It is wonderful what progress in invention can be made in a family of lively boys and girls wh. n free play is given to the imagination. They had already evolved out of their inner consciousnesses a truly remarkable craft, a home on the rolling deep that would not roll, a private house, with kitchen, parlor, dining-room, bedrooms, chambers, a piazza and back yard, on the deck of a timber float sixty by twenty. As no such craft had been ever described in ancient or modern history they were free to invent one in the usual happy American custom. After the manner of American marine architects they would make a boat unlike anything ever seen on sea or river. If America had produced the Sound Palace, the railway ferry-boat, the Western stern wheeler, and the Hudson River excursion boat, why should not the country bring forth a new style of marine cottage or floating summer residence.

The Professor finally brought the discussion to an end by saying that while the many suggestions offered were wise and altogether lovely, they must be guided by the fact that the boat was only sixty feet long over all. They must therefore content themselves to sleep two or even three in a room, the parlor and dining-room must be in one, and the lawn and croquet-ground must really be given up. The parlor must be at the bows to catch the breeze, and the kitchen must be at the stern.

On the following morning brother-in-law Snow, of Snow, Scauldfield & Butterworth, was asked by telephone if the timber-float could be hired for the summer, and he promptly replied that it could be secured till October for twenty-five dollars a month. It was a telephonic bargain, and at three o'clock that afternoon the Professor and his boys and girls met at the Thirty-fourth Street Ferry. The boys had each an old suit under his arm, while Patience and Sylvia carried lunch-baskets—a merry party bound over the ferry in search of good health and applied mechanics.

It was a queer craft, a mere wooden scow, or barge, lying partly in the river and partly in the black and ill-smelling mud. The stern was full of rain-water, and the bow, that was high and dry, had a bad crack. A carpenter had been engaged by telephone to repair the damage, and was at work when they arrived. The boys put on their

old suits, and with pails and dippers began to bail
out the boat, while the girls sat on the deck and
encouraged them by lively remarks on the antici-
pated voyage. Happily the tide was rising, and,
released of its load of water, the craft actually got
afloat just as the carpenter finished plugging up
the leak. Already the sun was sinking over the
city, throwing the buildings, chimneys, and spires
into dead purple shadow against the rosy west,
while the ships sailing past over the blue river
seemed to hang out crimson sails. There was even
a silver moon in young crescent in the sky, and the
Professor took it as the text for a brief and lumi-
nous talk on the tide and the moon.

"So," said Master Melancthon, "that bow of a
moon up there pulled our ship out of the mud.
It's real good in you, Mister Moon—much obliged,
I'm sure."

Just then little Sylvia gave a cry of delight.

"Oh! Look! See the steamer."

They all stood up on the edge of the boat and
looked out on the broad smooth river, flashing in
blue and purple in the sunset. On came, in swift
and silent majesty, one of the great Sound steamers,
glowing in white paint and quite resplendent in
the flags of all nations. It swept up the river, a
vast and mighty structure, instinct with life, throwing fantastic shadows over them as it went by.
Aloft stood the solemn look-out, and the three

pilots looking straight ahead, while from the guards
and balconies ladies and children looked down on
the odd little party on the scow. A great green
wave swept out from the surging wheels, turning in
rhythmic precision in their foam-decked houses.
The sun seemed to flash straight through the flag
streaming from its mast at the stern, and lit up the
ethereal rosy mist that seemed to linger after the
boat had gone. The green wave swept nearer and
nearer, and passed under the old boat, and lifted it
with a slow and solemn motion that they all said
was perfectly delightful.

Then they had lunch on a pile of boards in the
lumber-yard, and after that a man brought a bucket
of coal-tar and some well-worn brushes, and the
Professor and his boys went to work painting the
scow inside and out. It was quite dark when the
merry party went home over the ferry toward the
city, sparkling with a hundred twinkling lights, and
well pleased with their first taste by anticipation
of the delights of a voyage on a Sanitary Measure.

It is believed that the ideas of Professor Scantacre contain much of the greatest scientific value,
and that the truly original manner in which he and
his family went to sea and yet stayed at home, deserves the careful attention of the house-keeper, the
sanitarian, the navigator, and the philanthropic well-
wisher of the race. Therefore, at the risk of being
dull, the historian of the Voyage of the Sanitary

Measure must draw attention to details of construction. The Ark constructed by Commodore Noah has been described with considerable minuteness. This craft, too, sailed in search of new lands, where colds are unknown and fevers cease from troubling, and it is but right and proper it should be minutely described. There may never be a second flood, but a ship chartered in search of good health deserves all the eloquent and graphic language of a patent right.

The Professor and his boys, assisted by the kindly moon, hauled the craft high on the shore and blocked it up level, and then proceeded to finish painting their second-hand clothes and the boat. This done, floor boards were procured, and with saw and hammer they set to work, girls and all. Light beams were laid over a space of eleven feet at the bows, and on this was placed a deck, projecting two feet on every side, the over-hang being supported by extensions of the floor-beams. This they called the forward deck. At the stern they laid a deck three feet wide, but without any over-hang. This they said would be the back yard. Between these decks was a space forty-five feet long, and in this they laid a floor directly on the ribs of the boat. Four good casks were stowed away under the forward deck for water-tanks. Then between the two decks they set up, along each side, a row of 2 × 3 inch scantling, 7 feet long, and

securely nailed each to the side of the boat. At
the ends were somewhat longer uprights, and on
top of these were laid string-pieces and rafters of
the same material, and tied together by light
wooden strips, thus making a roof overhanging
the sides about two feet, so that the drip would
fall clear of the boat. The roof was covered with
cheap boarding, and was then covered with shingles,
while the ridge was finished off with a finial that
Sylvia cut out of pine on her scroll saw.

The Professor was a wise man. He had said,
" my boys and girls shall learn to use their eyes
and hands. They shall be able to drive a nail
straight and saw a board square, as well as con-
gugate Latin verbs." Indeed, he had once said
that one boy who could use tools was worth ten
who could write Latin verses, and who didn't know
a right-handed screw from a variable cut-off. Never
had children such a glorious time, the setting up
the posts of the house was a delight, hanging the
roof-tree a poetic joy, shingling the roof, to make
"from storms a shelter and from heat a shade,"
the greatest fun ever invented. Even the girls
helped lay the shingles, and Sylvia insisted in having one run through the middle, "swallow-tailed,"
on her fret-saw. The sides and ends they covered
with matched boards, leaving spaces for the doors
and windows. They hung glazed sash on hinges on
the outside to close over the openings, while two

plain doors made all tight and the house was com-
plete. The whole affair was painted white at
the sides and ends, and the roof was given a
coat of deep red while the hull of the boat was
black.

A cheap wall-paper was tacked to the tie-rods
of the roof, making a ceiling for the house, and the
space between the sides of the boat and the house
was covered with a heavy manilla paper, as a sort of
dado, which the girls afterward cleverly decorated
in red paint by the aid of a stencil. Then the
Professor and the boys set up thin partitions of
matched boards, dividing the house into a large parlor the whole width of the boat, at one end six
chambers, on each side, with a hall between, and a
kitchen and a bath-room. All the doors were left
as mere spaces to be closed by curtains, and the
wood was then neatly painted in pale green. Patience and Deliverance were specially busy with
brush and stencil, and carried a pretty band of color
round the upper part of the wall in the parlor. The
other rooms were simply left plain, and last of all,
the boys put up lots of nails and hooks for hanging
pictures, shelves, and clothing. Then the whole
affair was turned over to Mrs. Professor and the
girls, to do with as they would.

Of course the thing soon got into the papers.
Prying reporters came over to watch the building
of the ship. Some said the Professor was going to

live on the high seas to avoid paying taxes.
Others had the wit to see it was a germinal idea,
suggested by the Lake dwellers, the ancient Chi-
nese, and the modern Dutch, and that from it might
be evolved in due time a new style of habitation,
destined to remodel the home life of the American
people. A hotel clerk, with the instincts of his
cruèl race, saw in the floating house the doom of
his trade and sounded an appropriate wail in the
papers; but a confiding public refused to believe
in him or his wail.

Beds and furniture, a cook-stove and the kitchen
tools, china, and the bed and table linen, were sent
over on Monday morning and put on board.
Brother-in-law Snow loaned a good safe row-boat,
on the condition that he and his wife should have
the spare room Saturdays and Sundays, and even
permitted a young waterman, sometimes employed
about the yard, to ship as navigator and general assistant. A tug going down the bay was engaged
to take the house to Sandy Hook, and with the
cook, the navigator, and all the boys on board, it
sailed away between the two cities for the open sea.
The rest of the family packed up and took the Jes-
sie Hoyt for Sandy Hook at four o'clock, leaving
the house in charge of the second girl. When the
steamer finally pulled up at the lonely railroad pier,
there lay the new house at anchor off the beach,
half a mile away.

The baggage was placed on the pier, and officious persons connected with the railroad were for checking it for somewhere by the cars. No one save the light-house people were ever known to stop there with trunks and ladies, and it required some persuasion to convince them the family were really going no farther. The train steamed away over the beaches for Long Branch, and there they were, alone on the pier. The boys could be plainly seen in the front yard of the new house and the navigator was pulling away in the row-boat.

To the east were the dark and sombre pine-woods and the wastes of sandy beaches, with the two light-house towers against the pale sea sky. To the south the noble hills of Neversink, stretching away to the west, clothed in unbroken forests, save where a land-slide had scarred the hills with a splendid dash of warm rich red. To the west and north stretched the great bay, sea touching sky between the Jersey shore and Staten Island, where the sun was already declining in a rosy glow. There were ships at anchor all about, and to the north was an ocean steamer just turning the point and making for the sea, past the Hook. There were the gray forts at the Narrows, the white hotels at Locust Point, and far away a white steamboat, her many windows glittering in the sun. Nearer there was a steam yacht coming down under sails, wing in wing, in black silhouette against the sky. The

steamboat had left the pier and made a wide circle
as she turned back toward the city. The air had
fallen, and it was calm and still, save for the cry of
wheeling gulls over-head and the booming of the
surf on the outer beach.

"And here we may live in all the silence and
wildness, and yet be at home," said the Professor.
"Come, girls, our carriage is below."

For a carriage they had a boat, and for coach-
man, the family navigator. First the ladies were
taken over, and then a trip was made for the luggage. For once words failed the Professor's
family. They could not express their admiration
and satisfaction at this their new home, their cottage on the sea. The broad deck at the bows was
like a wide piazza directly over the water. They
could look down into the limpid depths and see
the long fronds and waving fingers of the sea-
plants, swaying gently in the slow motion of the
spent waves that came in from the open sea. There
were also fish to be seen, a sight to charm a
naturalist and drive a boy wild with delight. All
this directly under the piazza before the front
door. The door stood invitingly open, and they
descended two steps into the parlor and dining-
room to find the table already set for supper, with
every one's chair and napkin in the right place as at
home. The room itself was a wonder of Japanese
art. There were inverted umbrellas on the ceiling

fans and hangings on the walls, cleverly hiding the woodwork and giving the place a bright and lively color, while for pictures there were the four open windows looking out on sea and land. Over the door leading to the chambers and kitchen was hung a gray army blanket, decorated in Turkey red, sewed on. The chamber doors were closed in the same way, and in each was a wash-stand, beds, and plenty of hooks on the walls. The beds were raised on blocks, so that the trunks could roll beneath out of the way, and each room had a large window opening directly on the water and shaded by the overhanging eaves. The boys' room was filled up with berths, one over the other, and hinged so that they could be folded up like the beds in a sleeping car. The kitchen was a gem, with lots of closet room under the after-deck. For china-closet there was a shelf laid under the dining-table, while a rack suspended by cords over the table held the glass.

"Of course," said Mrs. Professor, "the house is very small, but then it is home."

Never did family sit down to supper under their own roof-tree amid such glorious surroundings. The sweet breath of the sea filled the room. The musical lapping of the tide against the boat, the faint cries of the gulls and the children's laughter mingling with the cheerful rattle of the silver. The Professor sat with his back to the Atlantic, and

3

mother sat with the hills of Neversink for a back-
ground to her happy face.

Only Patience was at all quiet. She had pulled
out the marine glass and taken a long look at the
steam yacht from her chamber window. It was
the Sylphide. To-morrow the fashionable party
on board would be sure to see this queer ark, and
would perhaps come over to inspect it. The
thought did not make her wholly happy.

After tea they spent the evening on deck, with
the great eyes of the lighthouses staring in the
most friendly manner at them. At last they all
slept in peace and security, with every window
wide open, and lulled by the musical roar of the
booming surf on the beaches beyond the silent
woods.

At half past four o'clock the next morning Master Melancthon Scantacre crawled out of his snug
berth and looked out the chamber window.

" Hurray, boys ! There's a whole fleet of
steamboats all round the house."

There was no more peace in that room, and, like
a troop of young colts, they scuttled into their
sailor suits, rushed through the house, and out on
the deck. Such a wonderful sight. The sun was
just rising over the woods, and the sky was still
flecked with rosy clouds. Six large steam fishermen had come in during the night and were
anchored near. There were also fourteen schooners

and five sloops, and all filled with men busy getting out great heaps of brown nets. On the deck lay a pile of mackerel, shimmering with all the colors of the rainbow and still alive. Near by stood the Navigator, fish-lines in hand.

" Now, me hearties, ye ken just keep quiet. The mackerel struck in the bay and there's going to be some fun. By mighty! Here they are agin ! "

Suddenly the water broke into foam all about them, millions of fish swept in clouds under the house, turning their glistening sides to the light as they went flashing by. No more sleep in that house. The entire family were promptly on deck to see the wonderful sight. Ah ! then there was excitement. The steamboats tripped their anchors and came careering round and round the house. Every craft sent out one or more boats. The fish were caught in a mass. There were shouts and cries on every side, frantic rowing and hauling in nets. Splendid blue-fish leaped out of the water in pursuit of their helpless prey. There were streaks of blood in the sea where they flashed through the water. Countless gulls seemed to suddenly gather over the foaming water. Not even the steamers could frighten them away, for it was a grand harvest of death for bird and fish and men. The family stood, as it were, in the midst of the slaughter. The Navigator with a long spear

occasionally landing a fat fish on the deck, while
the two older boys had a line each, and with shouts
and laughter brought in the glittering prizes as fast
as possible.

Suddenly it was all over. Not a fish to be seen.
Nothing but the limpid water and the waving
fronds of the algæ. The steamers came to their
anchorages again and the laden nets were hauled
in and made secure.

"They's struck off agin," remarked the Navigator. "Something scart 'em. Shall I clean up
some fish for breakfast, mum?"

"Breakfast!" said Mrs. Scantacre. "Yes. It
will take a dozen to supply the family if their appetites are equal to mine."

The Sanitary Measure had begun to work. It
required fourteen number two mackerel to supply
the family. And such a breakfast! As Patience
said, the language was wanting in tone; it could
not do justice to the event.

Mrs. Scantacre was alarmed. To supply the
larder with such a strain would be difficult.

"Never mind," said the Professor, "the sea
shall be our larder."

Just as they were rising from the table, the Navigator put his head in the front door and said:

"There's a lot of fellows out here, Captain, as
want to know what you call it anyway."

The entire family adjourned in a body to the

deck to see what this might mean, and found sixteen row-boats and dories, containing half a hundred fishermen, drawn up before the piazza. They were staring in the greatest curiosity at the strange craft, and when four ladies in morning toilets, a party of city children, and a learned Professor appeared, their amazement was unbounded.

An ancient mariner, with a ring of white hair round his face, and looking much like a grizzly saint whose halo had fallen down under his chin, took off his hat and said respectfully :

"I say, Capt'n, what do you call this ere craft? We aint seen nary sich a floatin' consarn—since the Ark."

"It's called the Sanitary Measure," said the Professor, in his most solemn manner.

This seemed to awe the entire company, and they began to whisper among themselves.

"Won't you come on board, gentlemen. My wife will be glad to show you the house."

They needed no second invitation, and literally swarmed into the house. Mrs. Professor apologized for the appearance of her establishment, as it was really so very early nothing was yet in order. The girls showed the visitors everything from pantry to parlor, and they in turn admired everything and said so in a truly frank and nautical manner.

"It's the tallest idee afloat! Just beats the hotels all to shoestrings. Heftiest kind of a sum-

mer house ever seen. Regular floating palace.
Sort of hearthstone on a raft. Guess the children
won't be took much with the diptheree in sich a
house. Ye ken just sit under yer own vine and
fig tree, and sail round independent, and go fishing
out yer parlor window."

These and other equally admirable compliments
were bestowed upon the house. One sharp-witted
fellow said :

"I swon if I don't fit up a house like this next
summer and take boarders ! It would just ruin
the Beach House at Squam Neck."

It was more than an hour before the jolly company departed to their several steamboats and
schooners, deeply impressed with all they had
seen. Then the Navigator took the Professor and
the younger children off in the boat, leaving the
Professor at the dock to take the steamer to town
and then landing on the beach that the boys and
girls might have the run of the woods and shore.
Aunt Jane said to Patience that it was time to put
the house in apple-pie order, as it was plain the
Sanitary Measure was an object of curiosity, and
that more visitors might be expected. Patience
suggested that "ship shape" would be a more
appropriate term for such an establishment.

The caring for the house was an easy matter.
There were no stairs to climb. Everything was as
convenient as a flat. They had the pure cold

water of the sea for washing purposes, and the
sanitary arrangements in regard to drainage were
intrusted to the resistless force of the tides that
swept under the house. The household cares finished, Patience sat down in the dining room alone
to her work. No idle embroidery, no silly " tat-
ting " or crazy " art-work " for this girl. Life was
too valuable for even plain sewing. She had other
materials—wood, brass, and glass. She had boys'
tools and was making a scientific apparatus of the
most singular construction ; thinking out its laws
in her mind, putting it together with her own
hands.

Suddenly Aunt Jane came into the room and
said in an excited whisper :

" Mercy ! Patience. There's a whole boat-load
of ladies and gentlemen coming over from that
yacht. I saw them from my chamber window."

Poor Patience knew her trial had come. How
could she receive Mr. Trefoil, and his fashionable
friends, in such a dreadful—dreadful thing ! Why
had her father exposed her to such humiliation ?

" I think," said her Aunt, " that it shows an independent spirit, and if these creatures laugh at my
brother's house I shall show them I don't care."

" Oh ! It's different with you. I know some
of these people. It's Mr. Trefoil's yacht. I saw
it come in last night and I was afraid he would call
on us."

Just then there came through the open window the sound of oars and a shout of merry laughter.

"They are laughing at our ridiculous house already."

"Well, never mind, if they have come to scoff they may remain to dine."

"Oh, I hope not, for there's nothing but fish to-day. I suppose I must go on deck and receive them."

As she came out of the little house and stood on the clean white deck, with a gorgeous Japanese umbrella over her head, she made a charming picture. The long yawl, rowed by four young sailors in fancy nautical suits, came swiftly over the long swinging rollers that swept in from the sea. In the stern sheets sat four young ladies and three young gentlemen, also in costumes that were at once ultramarine and altogether lovely. With a merry peal of laughter and a highly naval flourish of the oars the boat drew up 'long side. A young person in a fashionably marine suit stood at the stern and said :

"Good morning, Miss Scantacre. This is indeed a surprise."

Her face seemed to wear a decided pink. It might have been the glow of the red umbrella, or pride—or something else. She stepped to the edge of the deck and said with spirit :

"Good-morning, Captain Trefoil. I'm glad to

meet you upon the high seas, and much obliged
for the high nautical honors you have extended to
our ship. Please bring your honorable messmates
on board the Sanitary Measure."

The fashionable creatures in the boat were puzzled. Would it be the proper thing to recognize a
pretty girl living in a shanty on a scow, or would
they be justified in making sport of the whole
affair. Mr. Trefoil was evidently acquainted with
the young person, and though it was clear she was
very, very peculiar, it would not do to treat her
with rudeness.

"Is this the yacht of which you spoke, Miss
Scantacre?"

"It's not a yacht at all. It's only a Sanitary
Measure."

"A what, Miss?"

"This is the Sanitary Measure, Professor Scantacre Sailing Master, of New York, and bound on a
voyage in search of good•health. The captain's
gone to town, and the entire crew are ashore, or I
would receive you with naval honors, but mother's
at home and she'll be glad to see you."

One of the sailors let down the bar at the gang-
way, and with ill-suppressed merriment the young
people came on board and were duly presented by
Mr. Trefoil as some of his friends staying with him
on his yacht, now anchored off shore. Patience
was naturally a brave girl, but the reception they

3*

gave her was almost as much as she could bear. She knew they were laughing at her and at her father's house. She gave no look or sign of her hurt, nor of the righteous indignation that filled her heart. What right had these empty creatures to sneer at her father's sensible and independent method of spending the summer? The old fishermen were far more polite. She cast one appealing look at Mr. Trefoil and he had the wit to understand it and resolved that the Sanitary Measure should become the fashion.

"Won't you come into the parlor?" said Patience, opening the door. "It's very warm out here in the front yard."

The company all laughed heartily at this, and Mr. Trefoil said:

"So you call this deck the front yard, Miss Patience?"

"Certainly. This is our summer cottage and we have all the modern improvements."

The moment they entered the pretty little parlor their covert sneers changed to admiration, and they were lavish in praise of every thing. Mrs. Professor came in and was presented to the company. Everything was shown to them from parlor to kitchen, and they were more than pleased with all they saw.

Society can seldom go far in admiration, as its supply of good serviceable words is limited. The

Sanitary Measure was decidedly the thing. Society approved of the Professor's idea.

"Oh! it's not the Professor's idea," said Mrs. Scantacre. "It's an adaptation of the Lake Dweller's house. Thousands of families live afloat in China, and even on our Hudson there are many people who are born and brought up on canalboats. Why should we not keep house on the water? It's very quiet and healthful, and that's just what we want for the children."

"But your mansion can't sail," said Mr. Trefoil. "Here you are at anchor and here you must stay."

"Oh, indeed we can," replied Patience. "We can hire a tow-boat to take us from place to place, or we can put up a sail and go about on our own responsibility."

"I'm afraid, Miss Patience, the Sanitary Measure would sail majestically sideways with the wind abeam."

"Oh, no! I tell father he has only to put an outside centre-board on each side of the hull, just as I have seen in pictures of Dutch fishing-boats, and then we can steer her any where with a long oar."

"My dear," said Mrs. Professor to Patience, "take away your apparatus and we will have some lunch. I'm sure our friends must be hungry, for the Professor says the Sanitary Measure should be called the house of good appetites."

"Wait a moment, Miss Patience," said Mr. Trefoil. "Let us see the machine. What do you call it?"

"It is my heliograph," said Patience, displaying the curious apparatus on which she had been at work. It consisted of a long and narrow piece of wood, at one end of which was set up a thin piece of pine having a hole an inch in diameter cut through it near the top. Behind this was a small plate-glass mirror mounted in a frame, the frame being supported at the sides by two arms on which it was pivoted, so that it would turn on its horizontal axis at the centre. These supporting arms were in turn supported on a wooden block, free to turn on a vertical axis passing through its centre. This gave the mirror two motions, one vertical, one horizontal. Patience, without affectation or display of superior wisdom, showed how it worked, and even added that she had made it herself.

"Who ever uses such a thing?" asked one of the visitors.

"Oh, they are used in our coast survey, and in the British army they are used as a means of telegraphing across the country. If you will come on deck I'll show you what it is for."

There's nothing so interesting in the world as to see real work done, particularly if a pretty girl is to do it, and the entire party eagerly followed the fair scientist out on the deck.

" Now," said she, standing on the deck in the open sunshine, and pointing to the shore, " the children are playing off there on the beach. I'll send them a message and perhaps we shall get a reply."

The party confessed they could not see the children at all. Mr. Trefoil swept the beach with his marine glass, and at last said he could see some children near a white boat on the beach, and by dint of much pointing and searching they all said they could make out something that looked like a boat a long way off on the shore. Patience rested the instrument on the edge of the rail, and kneeling on the deck peered through a tiny hole in the back of the mirror.

" I'm finding the range. When I can see the boat through the hole in the mirror, and through the sight in front, I know the centre of the mirror and the sight are in line with the distant object. Now I turn the mirror to the sun till the reflection falls on the sight and then I know the beam of reflected sunlight is thrown directly on the spot covered by the sight."

Nothing happened for a moment, and they stood watching the fair young heliographist skilfully tilting the mirror up and down with a curious jerky motion.

" Oh, I understand," said Mr. Trefoil. " You are using the Morse alphabet."

"Certainly," she replied, without looking up, "and if my brother sees me he will—ah! there it is."

Suddenly there blazed up a strange white star, apparently on the water near the dark woods. It flashed up twice and then disappeared.

"What does he say?" asked one of the ladies.

"Oh, nothing. He's only holding a pocket-mirror in his hand and flashing it in this direction in the hope we may see it. He cannot hold it sufficiently steady in his hand to spell out any words. If he had a heliograph we could talk together easily, though he is nearly a mile away."

Society was greatly pleased with the performance and generously applauded the fair scientist. Then they returned to the house to consider a lunch and to bid Mrs. Professor and Aunt Jane good-by. Mr. Trefoil contrived to have a good deal of Patience's company, and more than one of the lady guests was jealous. Mr. Trefoil was a good "catch." It was not possible he was going to be led away by any such peculiar young person as this poor professor's daughter. It was all very well while she was simply the hostess in this delightful little cottage on the sea, but as Mr. Trefoil's friend! Really, it could not be exactly approved. At last they took to their boat and went away toward the Sylphide.

As the three ladies stood on the sunny deck to see them off, Patience remarked to her mother that she had been invited to dine on the yacht, and asked what she had best wear on that important occasion.

"Your regular marine suit, my dear. These steam-yachts are sometimes dreadfully dirty."

"It is clear," remarked Aunt Jane, as she watched the boat pull away, "that Society approves of the Sanitary Measure."

At noon the children were heliographed and bidden come home to lunch. And such a lunch! It was fortunate the Navigator made such a haul of fish. Mrs. Professor remarked on viewing the table that if good appetites were a sign of good health the Sanitary Measure was indeed a success. Then the children went off with the Navigator to hunt for clams at low tide, and the ladies of the family had the quiet house to themselves. Mrs. Professor fell asleep on the lounge in her room, Aunt Jane had some sewing in her own chamber, and Patience made herself comfortable over a novel in the parlor. Both windows and doors were wide open, and the sweet breath of the sea played with her light hair and made the gorgeous Japanese maidens on the walls flutter as if stirred by jealousy for the fairer maiden on the sofa. As for the cook she took her knitting to the back-yard, and sat down in the shade of the little house, remarking to herself,

"It's a quare place, anyhow, but mighty convenient to the water."

On board the Sylphide there was less happiness. The young people being thrown upon their own resources, soon became intensely stupid. Why did not their host hoist up anchor and continue the voyage? What was the use of staying in this lonely place? Mr. Trefoil was silent and preoccupied. He sent off a man to telegraph to the city for a certain book, a "Guide to the Telegraph." It came down by the last boat, and long after his guests had retired to their gorgeous and ill-ventilated staterooms he sat up studying the book. It may be also added to his credit that he committed the entire Morse alphabet to memory before morning.

Meanwhile we must return to the Sanitary Measure, for other events came to turn aside the whole current of the young man's life. In the midst of her reading Patience heard the sound of oars, and a boy's voice called out:

"Ship ahoy!"

She laid down her book, and putting on a big straw hat went out on deck. Along-side lay a heavy fishing-boat, and a small boy holding to the rail by one hand.

"Telegram, Miss. It came to the station and the man asked me to row off and bring it to yer. It's only a quarter."

She took the message, paid the boy, and was

turning away to go into the house when she paused, and asked the boy to wait as there might be a reply.

It was a message from her father to her mother, and saying that Cousin Mary's little boy at Troy was very sick and had been ordered to Manhattan Beach, but that he would, instead, be brought down by the early afternoon boat. Peter must be ready with the boat at the pier. Patience at once undertook to call the children home that the boat could be sent to the pier. When she came out on deck she looked off toward Staten Island, and saw that the afternoon steamboat was already almost at her pier. It was useless to call the boat home. It would take half an hour or more to get the boat to the house, leave the children, and start for the wharf.

"Boy, can you row me over to that steam-yacht?"

"Dunno, miss. I'm awful tuckered now. The boat is heavy, and I had to row mor 'n a mile to get here."

"Never mind. Pull up 'long-side. I'll take the oars. Now, sit at the stern and steer for the yacht."

The crazy old boat seemed to fly over the blue water, driven by strong young arms bent on an errand of mercy. They all seemed asleep on the Sylphide. There was no one in sight save an old man splicing a rope at the bows.

"Ship ahoy!" called a cheery voice over the water.

"Boat ahoy, there!" said the man. "What ken I do for ye, Captain—lady?"

"I want to see Captain Trefoil," said Patience, laying her boat 'long-side the steamer, and cleverly shipping her oars in reach of the boy.

"Lend a hand, Bo'sun. I want to come on deck."

"Here ye have it, miss. Jump, now. There ye are. I'll call the Cap'n."

Brilliant with the color caused by her exertion, her eyes sparkling with excitement, and dressed in some blue stuff that with her big straw hat seemed to make a frame, she seemed a marine sketch worthy a master. Mr. Trefoil came on deck, surprised and charmed.

"Delighted to see you, Miss Scantacre. To what do I owe this pleasant visit?"

"A Sanitary Measure, sir."

Then she briefly explained that she wanted four good men and a fast boat to bring the sick child from the pier to the house.

"I'm very sorry, miss. My men have gone to the pier to meet the steamboat to get some luggage that's coming down. Hold on! there's the steam-launch. Is steam up, Bo'sun?"

This was to the man, and he went over to the other side where a pretty little steam-launch lay along-side. He slid down to her and looked at the tiny boiler.

"Yes, sir, there's a little on. We can get up more in half a jiffy."

"Oh, that will do, sir!" said Patience. "See, the steamer is hauling up to the pier. Let's go at once."

"Call the engineer, Bo'sun."

"He's not here, sir. He went ashore with the men."

"Never mind, I can run the engine. Here, little boy, here's some money for you; I shan't want your boat." This was to the boy, who took the money and pulled lazily away.

"But really, Miss Patience, you cannot do it; you will be sure to soil your hands."

"Never mind my gloves. They are old. Come, help me down, Bo'sun."

She took the leap cleverly and landed on the forward deck of the launch, ran along to the little engine-room and looked in.

"Come on, Mr. Trefoil, I'll be the engineer. Close the furnace door, Bo'sun, and cast off the bow-line. Do come, sir, the steam's rising fast!"

Mr. Trefoil had at times certain doubts as to the mental stability of the young girl who stood at the door of the engine-room, gravely wiping the handle of the reversing bar with some cotton-waste.

Might she not blow the whole thing up, sink the boat, or at least disarrange the machinery?

"She's an A 1 engineer, and I dare say she's a master's certificate in her pocket," remarked the bo'sun.

"Please come, sir. The poor child may be very, very ill on the pier. I must go to him. More coal, Bo'sun."

With that she turned to the boiler, tried the steam, and started the pump, and began to warm up the engine for its work. Mr. Trefoil was ashamed and vexed that he hesitated, and without a word slid down the rope to the stern of the launch, and cast her off. At the instant the quick puff of the engine startled him, and the wheel churned the water into foam under the stern.

"Port your helm, Mr. Trefoil."

"Port it is, engineer. Full speed ahead."

The fussy little boat shot away from the yacht, and described a half-circle over the water and started away for the dock. Society, startled out of its nap by the engine, came on deck only to see their elegant host steaming away with a strange girl in a big hat.

"Gracious!" said one lady. "Dear Mr. Trefoil said we could not use the launch without the engineer."

"The lady seems to be running the engine,"

remarked a young gentleman, who was peering through a glass at the launch.

" It must be that strange girl from the Professor's ark. She's very peculiar. I am not sure that we ought to recognize her in town."

Fortunately the steamboat landed her passengers quickly and backed off from the dock, thus leaving it clear for the launch that came plowing through the creamy water under her bows. The passengers, eager to get on, took to their train and went away toward Long Branch. Mr. Trefoil's men found the luggage, and, piling it on board their boat, rowed away for the yacht before he observed them, and by the time the launch shot under the piles of the pier they were beyond hail. As the boat stopped at the foot of the slippery wooden steps Patience sprang out and began to run up the wet stairs. It was a dangerous business, and she was glad to wait a moment and take Mr. Trefoil's arm up to the pier.

It was a sorrowful sight. The child lay upon a litter, pale and still, while a young man knelt beside it, holding an umbrella over its face and testing its feeble pulse. Near by stood a woman leaning on the Professor's arm and weeping silently. Patience slipped away from Mr. Trefoil and went to her cousin, while he reverently took off his hat and stood watching the scene.

" Oh, Cousin Patience, he is dying ! he is dying !

I brought him down the river by express and through the city. He became like this on the boat. It's all in vain. He cannot live."

" Oh, no ! no ! He will revive in this air. There ; take my arm. Come, he must be put to bed at once."

" Where can he go in this wild place ? There's not a house near."

" Father, ask some of the railroad men to help us. There's a boat at the foot of the stairs. Come cousin, let us take him home at once."

Mr. Trefoil stepped forward and offered his help. He was learning much of this strange girl. Here was a new side to her many-sided character. One of the railroad men touched his cap and said to Patience :

" The boys will lend a hand, miss. We'll take the child to the boat."

So it was they went down to the boat. The Professor and the young doctor from Troy, the station-master and a brakeman with the child, Patience and her cousin following behind, assisted by Mr. Trefoil. The bo'sun had turned the launch round and it lay with the stern to the steps. The litter was placed on the floor of the stern sheets and they all got aboard. Some one started the engine and some one else took the tiller, and the boat with its sorrowful freight shot away swiftly for the Sanitary Measure. It came on full speed, reversed suddenly, and cleverly swung up 'long-side the forward deck. Capital navigation that ! Mrs. Professor and Aunt Jane were on deck, ready to receive the child, and the gentlemen, assisted by the bo'sun, took the little fellow to the spare room and laid him upon the bed by the open window. The young doctor looked about in amazement. Never in all his experience had he seen such a wonderful hospital, such a union of pure sea air and solid domestic comfort. It was a sanitary inspiration. The child would live.

Mr. Trefoil, not wishing to intrude on the sorrowful household, took himself and his man to the deck as soon as the child had been placed upon the bed, and waited. More than half an hour passed and still he sat on a camp-stool looking absently off on the sea and thinking of the might be. The bo'sun sat in the launch, keeping up steam and thinking—of supper. Suddenly Patience came out on deck with the heliograph in her hand.

" Oh, Mr. Trefoil ! I didn't know you were waiting. We are in such sad trouble about the poor child I—I quite forgot you. You are very kind to lend me the launch."

" You're very welcome, Miss Patience, and I'm dreadfully mortified to be obliged to ask of you a favor in return."

" Why, certainly, sir. What can I do ? "

" I would like to go home, but you see—you won't laugh at me, please—"

His handsome face wore a look of mingled amusement and mortification.

"My predicament would—would be positively funny—if it were not so dreadfully humiliating. I can't get home."

"Why not ? There's the launch."

"That's just it. My people on the yacht will not send for me because they know I have the launch. Oh, you may laugh ! I deserve it. My education has been sadly neglected. I really don't know how to handle the engine and I dare not trust the bo'sun."

"Excuse me, sir. It is rather funny. Just wait till I call the children and I'll take you home."

She went to the edge of the deck, adjusted the heliograph, and in exactly ten seconds the children who were loading their boat with a magnificent cargo of clams, a mile and a half away, said among themselves :

"Sister is calling. It's time to go home."

The bo'sun took the tiller, and the young Society man and the learned daughter of science sat in the little engine-room with the pretty engine between them.

"Seems to me you are driving her full speed."

"Yes. She's doing her best."

"I think half speed would be nicer."

She put her hand on the lively engine and it

calmed down and assumed a slow and dignified pace, making a rhythmic cadence to a pair of fast-beating hearts. Love tells its tale now-a-days in strange places, and this time the story begun in a marine engine-room off Sandy Hook.

The bo'sun observed the slowing down of the boat's speed and remarked to himself :

" This yere female engineer is running this thing on the principle that the longest way round is the sweetest way home."

Society on the Sylphide was petrified. Mr. Trefoil in a launch with a young person of the most singular habits !

" No doubt she's really some fireman's daughter. The Professor's family must be mere working people. Some of Mr. Trefoil's friends should speak to him about it. The poor young man would be sadly entangled by the designing creature. I'm not sure that we ought to recognize her."

These things they said in their hearts as the launch came along-side. Outwardly they wore, after their manner, a smiling face and most gracious aspect.

Mr. Trefoil was breaking through the crust that had grown over his heart. He had learned much in that little engine-room, and, in spite of certain meaning glances, he helped his fair engineer on board and invited her to stay to dinner. Patience with all her science was a woman and instantly grasped the whole situation.

4

"Thank you, sir ; I must go home to my cousin Mary. If you will let your men take me back I shall be greatly obliged."

Mr. Trefoil urged her to stay, but she would not. The long yawl was brought round and four stout men took the oars. Patience sat at the stern with the tiller ropes in her hand and waved a farewell to the yacht. The men pulled fast and strong and she steered straight away for home, with eyes fixed dreamily on the purple hills, the glowing sky, the sombre woods of the Hook, and the level sea glowing in the sunset. Swift over the water flew the boat bearing this fair young scientist, this charming engineer, but with all her skill she had not been able to bring away her heart. She had left it on the yacht.

This is the record of one day on the Sanitary Measure. To tell of all the days that followed would fill a book. The chief point to be regarded is that the floating house was really a sanitary measure. In twenty-four hours the sick child was able to sit up ; in another day it was much better, and within one week it could sit out on the sunny piazza, while Master Melancthon caught crabs for its amusement. The doctor was in ecstacies over the floating hospital. It had undoubtedly saved the child's life. He must read a paper on the subject before the Medical Society. It even got into the papers, and within a week a gentleman applied for a room in the house for his sick wife. He would pay anything, a hundred dollars a week for a single room in a house that was better than medicine. The family could not receive him, for the house was full. Even the doctor had to sleep on a cot in the parlor and brother-in-law Snow had to omit his first Sunday in the marine mansion.

The skeptical reader may here remark that a child apparently dying would not thus recover merely by living on the sea in a comfortable house. In reply, it may be observed that often when the sick children are brought on board the floating hospital, belonging to the St. John's Guild of New York, apparently in a dying state, that, if they manage to live for half an hour, or till the boat is clear of the city, they often completely recover. It is admitted that in such cases it is the change of air that saves the child's life, and ultimately effects a permanent cure.

The Sylphide meanwhile remained persistently at anchor off the steamboat landing, with her fires out and engine rusting. The gay party on board were thoroughly disgusted. They had come out on a cruise, and to be anchored in inglorious ease in smooth water was a trifle tiresome. Mr. Trefoil did not seem to care very much. He visited the Sanitary Measure often, and twice had Patience and one of her sisters to dine on the yacht. He even took the entire family on a trip out to sea for

a whole day, while his visitors were ashore upon
a visit to the city.

Then came a day of more notable events that
turned the entire current of two young lives, and
happily illustrated how, in these days, love may
call high science to its aid. Mr. Trefoil's guests,
wearied of their inactive life, had, with one excuse
or another, returned to their homes or gone to find
more lively resorts of fashion; and one warm
August day Mr. Trefoil found himself alone on his
yacht with his crew. It was nine o'clock in the
morning when he came out, and began to pace up
and down the deck, deep in thought and trying to
take a practical view of the situation. The sailing-
master and the engineer, with their men, were all
on deck watching their employer with some curiosity. What would he do next? Were they to
let the barnacles grow on the keel and see the
engine rust in idleness?

"Hallo, Mr. Engineer! How long will it take
to get up steam?"

"Forty minutes, sir."

"All right! Start up your fires. I say there,
Captain, have the launch brought round as soon
as you get her steam."

Then the young man went below to array himself in his best apparel; he must make himself as
presentable as possible on such an important occasion. Somehow his fingers trembled nervously,

and the whistling of the men on deck and the cheerful clamor in the boiler-room seemed to jar on his spirit. Perhaps he was out of tune with the world. His men were happy over their work, for they were earning money for others—for wives and little ones. What was the use of his gilded and idle life? It was certainly of no use to him. He too would try and do something for others. He would go over and see Patience and invite her to take—a long voyage. While busy dressing he looked out the port and saw that the morning boat from the city had pulled up at the wharf, discharged her passengers, and was backing off for the return trip. At the same time he saw a row-boat containing a woman, with something in her arms, starting off from the dock toward the Sanitary Measure.

"I hope she is not a visitor. I must contrive to see Patience alone, if possible."

The boat from the pier pulled up along-side the Sanitary Measure, and the Professor and his wife and daughter came out on deck to see who had arrived. It was a poor woman, a total stranger, from the city, appealing to them for help and pity. Her child, that she held in her arms, was very ill—in fact, it seemed as if it could not live many hours. She had read in the papers of the wonderful recovery of the little one from Troy while in the floating house, and in her poverty and despair she had brought her child down in

the blind hope that, for charity's sake, it could
be taken into the house. She was sure it would
live if only it could sleep in quiet and peace in a
house—on the sea. Would they take the child in
for a few days? She was a widow woman. It
was her only child.

The case appealed strongly to the Professor and
his wife, and they were sincerely sorry to tell the
woman they could not take her in. There were
other children and friends, some of them invalids,
staying at the house, and every bed was occupied
—in fact, the man had slept on deck for two nights,
and there were two cots in the parlor. In the
midst of this rather painful episode Mr. Trefoil's
steam-launch was seen approaching. Patience
guessed he might be coming to see her, and knowing she could do nothing to help the poor woman,
she entered the house and went to her own room.

Shortly after, her aunt came to the curtained
door to say that Mr. Trefoil was waiting in the
parlor to see her. She asked what had been done
about the poor woman and her child, and her aunt
replied that Mr. Trefoil had sent the woman and
child away in his steam launch—probably to the
dock to take the next boat to the city. It seemed
strange to Patience that he should do this, but in
her haste to go to him she attached no particular
significance to the incident and presently forgot it.

Patience drew the curtain aside, and entered the

parlor quietly and with perhaps a certain subdued and thoughtful expression on her face. The sad fate of the poor woman, forced to appeal to total strangers to save her child's life, and the utter impossibility of doing anything for her, had for the moment sent a chill over her spirits. Mr. Trefoil sat by the open window looking off on the wide bay, and she came quite near before he observed her. He turned quickly, and his eyes seemed filled with a new and strange light, as if he had just passed some peculiar experience, as if moved by some novel emotion.

Only a poet can tell a tale of love in the words in which it may be spoken. It is always a poem, even though words are not used at all. Whatever words were used on this occasion the fact remains that she refused him. Why? As well ask why the bee slights one flower for another. Did she love him? Yes. No. She was not sure. Something in his manner chilled her. He seemed in some sense conferring a favor, and she resented it. Fashionable life had formed a hard, indurated crust over him. He had just done a rather strange thing, and was laboring under some excitement. He was not sure whether she would praise or blame him, and it is quite possible he did not plead his cause with the warmth he might have shown under other circumstances.

The short puff of the steam-launch came in at

the open window, and in a moment after she felt the house jar as the awkward sailors let the boat strike the deck. It had come to take him back to his fashionable friends on his elegant yacht. His life seemed far removed from hers. She felt sure she could not love him.

She hardly knew how he left her. She knew he was bitterly disappointed and she could not look in his face, lest she relent, and only when she heard the exhaust of the engine as the launch steamed away, did she wake up to the fact that he had gone forever. She sat silent and depressed by the window, looking off on the sombre woods and the hot burning sands of the Hook, dreaming of the might be, and vaguely asking her heart if she had done right. Perhaps it was all a mistake, an irreparable blunder, to darken and cloud her whole life. More than an hour passed thus, and then with a heavy sigh she rose to go to her room. She would lie down awhile—to sleep, and forget this life so full of perplexities and disappointments.

Just at the moment her mother entered the room, and Patience, in default of anything else of which to speak, asked what had become of the poor woman and her child.

"Why, Mr. Trefoil had her sent to his yacht. I thought you knew it. It was certainly a very noble piece of charity in the young man. He quite won your father's heart."

And this was the man she had refused. While she had been thinking him hard and selfish, he had been doing a kindly action for a total stranger, had actually taken the widow and her child on his elegant boat, in the hopes that it too might prove a sanitary measure. She crossed the room, and looked out on the water. The yacht had gone. It had left its familiar anchorage, and was not anywhere to be seen. She took up the field-glass that hung by the window, and scanned all the wide reach of water, from the Narrows far along Staten Island to where sky and water met at the head of the bay. If he had sailed toward the city, or up the bay, he would not yet be out of sight. He must have gone to sea past the Hook. She threw the belt of the glass over her shoulder in nervous haste. Perhaps there was yet time to correct her dreadful mistake. She went to her room, took up the heliograph, tied on her big straw hat, and went hastily out on the deck, intending to call the boat home. Fortunately it was nearly noon, and the Navigator was just returning with the children. The moment they were safely on deck, she bid the man row her as fast as possible to the shore.

Now she saw his true character. The crust was only a crust, he was not all selfishness and conventionality. How she loved him! She was sure of it now, and perhaps it was all too late. The grat-

4*

ing of the keel woke her up to action, and in a moment she was upon the wet sand.

" Wait here, Peter, with the boat, till I return. I am going over to the outer beach."

She walked rapidly across the narrow strip of sand, crossed the railroad in the woods, even ran part of the way, and in a few moments came out on the white sloping beach close to the booming surf, and with the Atlantic spread wide before her. The moment she cleared the woods and came down on the shore, she stopped, panting and trembling, and raised the glass, and scanned the west horizon. A rosy blush mounted to her face. There was the Sylphide steering straight away to the East, with sails a-wing before the breeze, making, under steam and sail, full speed for the open sea. She kneeled down in the hot and glistening sand, took off her hat and carefully sighted the yacht with the heliograph. She glanced up at the friendly sun, as if to call him to her aid. Prehistoric maidens worshipped the Sun-god. She used the sun to tell a tale of love. It had already passed the meridian, and only with the greatest difficulty could she bring the mirror to reflect his rays to the east. She had forgotten to bring the second mirror needed when the sun is behind the operator using the instrument. Perhaps there was yet time. She took off her hat, and used it as a shield to cut off the beams of light sent far off to the yacht, and with quick motions, spelled out letter by letter, a strange love message flashed in sunlight over the sea.

. . . .

The yacht sailed on and on. The crew, pleased to end their inactive life at anchor, worked cheerily to send the splendid boat through the foaming water. The master had returned from his visit to the Sanitary Measure, silent, preoccupied, and apparently ill-natured. It is not in human nature to bear all things with serenity, particularly when one has every wish gratified save the greatest wish of all. Immediately on his return to the yacht, young Mr. Trefoil ordered the anchor up and steam made. He bid the sailing-master steer past the Hook for open water, and then he went below. The breeze was fair and sail was set as the boat rounded Sandy Hook and came out upon the apex of the vast triangle made by the Long Island shore and the Jersey coast, with the marine horizon for its base. Mr. Trefoil came on deck in a rough yachting suit and looked all about on sea and land. He seemed depressed and ill at ease, and it was some moments before the sailing-master dared speak to him.

" Where shall I lay the course, sir ? "

" Oh, I don't care. Anywhere. Go to sea—to Halifax if you like."

The sailing-master, blunt to such grim humor,

took the direction literally and went forward to the man in the wheel-house.

" Keep her two points north of east till we make Montauk to'ards midnight."

" Where are we going, Captain ? "

" Nova Scotia."

" All right, jolly long trip. Two points north it is."

Mr. Trefoil came slowly along the deck, looking absently off over the sea and trying to forget. Just by the mainmast the steward stepped up, touched his cap and said :

" The child seems to be better, sir. I did not take it below, for the boys rigged a hammock for'ard and put it in it."

" Oh ! I quite forgot the child. Let me see it."

The sailors with kindly skill had swung a hammock on the deck in the shade of the foresail, and wrapped a blanket round the child who lay in it. It seemed to be sleeping as the young man drew near, and its mother, who sat by its swinging bed, rose and stood beside it.

" He will live, sir, I feel sure of it. It's the sea air's a doing mor'n all the doctors. May God bless ye, sir, for taking pity on me."

" Oh, that's all right. Don't say anything about it. I'm sure you're very welcome. I hope it will soon be better."

He paused and stood looking at the thin and

wasted features of the child, and even smoothed
its hair that stirred in the pure salt air. His touch,
however gentle, woke the child and it looked up
in his face and smiled. Then it seemed to be restless and uneasy, and tried to sit up in its swinging
bed. The young man, little heeding his crew who
stood looking on in surprise, gently put his arm
under the child and raised him up. The child
even leaned his head on the young man's shoulder
in childlike confidence. If then there stirred in
his heart a bitter pang of regret and disappointment at the impossible "might have been," he
repressed it for the child's sake. He talked to it
pleasantly and assisted it to look far round on the
wide sea, the white hotels on Coney Island, fring-
ing the northern horizon like some strange city,
the blue hills of Neversink fast dropping astern.
The mother looked on in silent thankfulness and
happiness, wondering much at the wonderful
change in the child. It seemed another being, as
if the breath of the sea had given it new life. Suddenly the child's eyes brightened, and it pointed
with one thin hand astern toward the receding
shore.

"Oh! see, mother, see the pretty white star."

They all turned to look to the west. There, on
the verge of the horizon flamed and burned a great
white star. Ah! It was gone. No; there it
beams again. Gone again. It seemed to flash in

fitful starts, blazing up for a moment and then going out again.   Mr. Trefoil had been looking off to the south over the sea, and, until the child spoke, he did not see this singular star flashing like a tiny sun upon the horizon.   The moment he saw it he let the child fall back in its hammock and stood up.

"Port your helm—port, I say!   Let go that foresheet!   Look lively there!   Send down the jib on the run!   Keep her hard aport!   Bring her 'round lively!"

The men, startled by the abrupt commands, were a trifle dilatory, and the yacht swung round in a great circle.   The foresail flew back and jibbed over with a lurch that made the boat reel, while the jib came down on the run and dragged in the water.

"Take in all sail, Captain, and tell the engineer to give her more steam."

"What course shall I take?" said the perplexed wheelman, looking out his window.

"Steer for Sandy Hook—full speed ahead."

.   .   .   .

The sun, hastening to the west, refused to send another word by the heliograph.   She looked up at it in an agony of tears and disappointment.   What if he did not see her signal, what if he failed to notice her far-flashed message.   Why had she forgotten the second mirror. Perhaps all was lost, perhaps everything was in vain. She put up the marine glass and scanned the horizon and then took it down, for her hand shook and her eyes were blinded. The yacht had disappeared. It had gone below the horizon. Her message had been spent upon the barren sea. She never knew how long she sat on that lonely beach with the useless heliograph fallen on the sand at her feet. It must have been a long time, for the Navigator, becoming alarmed at her prolonged absence, crossed to the beach in search of her.

" Beg pardon, Miss Patience. I didn't know but you was lost."

"Thank you, Peter, it's nothing. I was not very well, and I sat here to rest."

It seemed as if she did not care for anything now, save for peace—peace and forgetfulness.

The man was perplexed for a moment and stood looking off on the sea. Then he said abruptly: " Beg pardon, Miss Patience, but I am thinking you'd best come home. There's the Sylphide just arounding Sandy Hook."

UNDER HIGH PRESSURE.

SAMUEL BREEWOOD came out of the Massachusetts Institute of Technology with the highest
honors. Some of his friends, it is true, had re-
gretted that he was not a Harvard man ; but he
was at all events a man who knew the use of tools.
He had no Greek and little of the classics, but he
was theoretically master of the steam-engine, the
machine lathe, the rock-drill, and those noble and
ancient tools—the file and hammer ; moreover, he
had learned the use of those finer tools—the brain,
the eye, and the hand ; and though practically he
knew little of real work, he said to himself that he
would soon bring his theory to the level of practice.

For a few weeks after leaving school he looked
about near Boston for something to do, and found
that the world somehow seemed already too full
of engineers. To make a moan over this, after
the manner of some who find their market over-
stocked, was not in his nature. He recognized
that to begin he must begin, and after some search

he at last obtained a place as clerk of the High Bush coal-mine at Emberton City, Pennsylvania.

To one brought up in the rarified intellectual atmosphere of Boston, Emberton City seemed stifling. The raw, straggling town, the squalid poverty of the mining population, the ill-made and inefficient machinery employed in the mines, and, above all, the ways and manners of the people, depressed him. He wanted to reform and improve everything in sight, from the miners' huts to the manners of their sons and daughters. Being wise, he did nothing of the kind, and contented himself with his clerical duties of keeping the accounts of the out-put of the mine and the wages of the men. He was an engineer, doing a clerk's duty, but he would bide his time till something more congenial offered.

He had taken lodgings with a widow woman named Baumgarten, who had one daughter aged nineteen. This place was the only one that had offered, and he had taken it on impulse.

To this *ennuyé* young man, not without certain disheartening experiences of "society," Maria Baumgarten seemed more completely a woman than any he had ever seen. He said to himself in an extravagant way, that he had not met a young woman before, but merely cultivated young persons of feminine aspect. She appealed to him with a vivid intensity and an open-air freshness that were entirely new to him, and it was not without an occasional feeling of surprise that he came to acknowledge a more decided feeling of genuine preference for her than he had thought again possible to him. How those young ladies he had known in Boston would have smiled had they seen him carrying her hymn-book as they walked on Sunday morning to the little wooden church, apparently well pleased to accompany a girl absolutely without " views " or " kulture ! " She could cook and sew, and these operations did not seem to impair her very decided beauty. She seemed to express life and high spirits and intense womanliness, as if it was a good thing to have limbs, to be able to run, to walk, to laugh and be alive.

To Maria Baumgarten, the Eastern man, with his thin, delicate features and quiet manners, seemed a new revelation. The ruddier sons of her native mountains lost their charm, and gradually she came to have nothing more to do with them. Rumor said that one of her lovers, a fine young fellow named Krumburger, employed in the High Bush pit, took it greatly to heart.

Weeks passed and matters progressed, and one March morning they came to a sudden climax.

It was Saturday morning, about twelve o'clock, when Breewood looked up from the High Bush company's ledgers, and gazed round the bare, white-washed room that constituted the company's office. The sanded floor, the ugly stove, the coal-dust

covering everything, the grimy windows, seemed
to fall upon him as a blight, a numbing weight of
unloveliness. Through the window he could look
out upon the mountain-side, torn and half denuded
of trees ; the enormous coal-breaker, black and
hideous in the sunshine ; the vast heaps of coal-
dust, the tangled skein of rude railway tracks, and,
above all, the pit's mouth, a dark spot on the
white, snow-clad mountain.

Suddenly he heard the steam-whistle at the
engine-house blowing furiously. The engineer
must have mistaken the hour : it was not yet noon.
While thinking of this, he saw a man running
down the tracks toward the town, and, at the same
time, noticed puffs of steam from the engine, as if
the hands were at work dragging up a load on
the trolley, a car that ran up and down the pit.
Something unusual had evidently happened.

Breewood closed the books hurriedly and went
to the door. The man came toward him, shouting and waving his arms in a frantic manner. As
he ran past the door, he cried out :

"Sweetbriar has bu'st inter High Bush. The
mine's floodin' ! "

Hastily locking his office, Breewood ran like a
deer over the snow-covered tracks toward the pit.
In a moment he saw an engine drawing out of the
breaker with a train of loaded cars, and he gave
the signal to stop. By the time he met the engine

it had stopped, and the engineer leaned out the window to see what was wanted.

"Take off your cars and run down to the station and telegraph to Pottsville for the superintendent. Say Sweetbriar has burst in, and order up two steam-pumps and a thousand feet of two-inch pipe and as much four-inch with couplings. Then bring your engine to the pit as soon as possible."

That the clerk should give orders in this manner puzzled the engineer, but he accepted the commission and quickly cast off his train and went flying down the crazy track at full speed.

By the time Breewood reached the breaker, its dizzy stair-ways were swarming with men and boys pushing and struggling to get up to the top floor, where they might take the high-level bridge to the pit's mouth. He had to take the longer path up the mountain, and by the time he reached the pit there was a frantic crowd of men swarming into the engine-room and about the huge black hole where the steep railway led down into the lower darkness of the mine. These mines are "on the slope," and the pit did not go down vertically, but at an angle of 45°. Just as he arrived, the trolley, drawn up by a wire rope, came to the surface, and a mingled shout and groan went up from the excited throng of men gathered round the pit's mouth. The trolley and its load made a horrid spectacle. It was choked with men, bleeding and torn, and crowded together in frightful confusion, who had fought in brutish selfishness for a chance to come up from the flood below. The trolley rolled up to the level, and a hundred hands were stretched to rescue them.

Breewood went into the engine-house. The place was deserted by the fireman and engineers, who had gone to see who had been saved. Indignant at this neglect in such an emergency, he went back to the door and called for the firemen.

A big fellow, black with coal-dust, shook his fist at him and cried :

" Who be you ? Be you the boss ? "

" No. But I mean to be. Go back to your work at once and raise more steam."

The man put his hands in his pockets and turned sullenly away. Breewood recognized that if anything was to be done he must be master. He looked out over the bridge and saw a thousand frantic men and women rushing in terror up the mountain-side. In a moment there would be a senseless and helpless mob, and, meanwhile, perhaps men were drowning in the darkness three hundred feet under the streets of the town. He went out on the platform about the pit's mouth, and springing upon the wooden rail, he shouted, as loud as he could, above the babble of voices :

" Lend a hand, men ! There may be more left below ! "

There was a momentary hush, and the men turned to see who spoke.

" They be dead," said some one.

" Then we must save the bodies. Come, men, lend a hand and we'll save them."

He would have said more, but there was a loud murmur of discontent. Who was this—this clerk with his fine hands? What did he know about mining? He must be a fool to think any one alive in the mine while the water filled the bottom of the slope.

" Lend a hand, men ; we can save them yet ! "

A grizzly-headed Welshman took off his hat and said respectfully :

" They be all dead, mister. It's no use doin' a thing."

There were murmurs of approval at this, but Breewood replied promptly :

" The men at the top of the slopes are alive. The air must keep the water away from them."

This remark won instant assent, and he followed up his advantage quickly.

" Come. I'm going down. Who'll go with me ? "

A dozen hands were raised, and Breewood jumped down from the rail and took command of the work ; and with that recognition that working-men always show to a mind that can lead, they waited for commands.

" Let the firemen go back to the work and get up extra steam. I've ordered up a pump. It will be here in a few hours."

Several men moved away toward the boiler-house, and the rest stood expectant and silent.

" I want a stone-hammer and three young men."

Several men stepped forward and Breewood selected his men, and some one having brought a stone-hammer, they four got upon the trolley and prepared to go down into the pit.

" Count the men, and see how many are missing. Let some of the men go home for their meals, and let a full set of tools be sharpened and made ready for work. Go ! "

At the word, the trolley rolled slowly down the steep incline and disappeared in the darkness. Then a hush fell upon the crowd of people gathered round, and they waited in silence till the signal should come up from below. Women and children were arriving from the village every moment, but they seemed awed into silence, and stood waiting for news. By that curious instinct that affects such crowds, they felt sure that some were still in the mine, but who or how many, or whether dead or alive, they could not say.

Ten minutes later the signal-bell rang and the steel rope began to creep up the slope. Instantly the crowd pressed nearer to get a view of the rising trolley. Suddenly bell rang to stop and a painful silence fell on the people. Then a woman began to sob, and then another, and in a moment several were crying.

"Whist ! woman !" said one to another. "Your man be all right. He's a-bossin' the job."

Then the bell rang again. The engine turned swiftly and silently, and in a moment the trolley rose into view, and the crowd struggled closer to get a view of its occupants.

Breewood was standing on the edge of the car, and as it came to the surface he said :

"They're alive ! Volunteers to the rescue !"

A wild shout of joy went up from the vast throng that had gathered round the pit, and a hundred voices suggested this thing and that, but Breewood held up the stone-hammer and commanded silence.

"We knocked and they replied to us. They are caught in the top of a slope. We must cut them out."

A dozen big fellows armed with picks stepped forward, eager for the work.

"Hold on, men. We must have a stage built first to work from, and a place for the pumps, for the water is rising fast."

"Oh, they'll be drowned, they'll be drowned !" screamed a woman in the crowd.

"No, they won't. They are perfectly safe till we reach them."

These words calmed the woman and prevented

the infection of excitement from spreading, and Breewood called for carpenters and a load of heavy timbers.

"Who are the missing men?" he asked.

"Dennis Nagle, John Smith, and John Krumburger," said a voice in the crowd.

A momentary flush of color spread over the young man's face, but he turned quickly away and hid it from them.

Timbers were quickly gathered and loaded into the trolley, and two men with heavy axes got in on top of the load. Breewood borrowed a foot rule from one of them, and carefully measured a length of rail on the railway. An old man who watched him, said:

"The last rail is a half one, sir."

"Ah! yes, thank you. I was measuring the distance from the top of the pit. I counted the rails we passed. One hundred and sixty-eight feet from the top is the place for the stage."

"Yes, sir; and one turn of the winding-drum takes you down twenty-eight feet."

"Good! That's just the information I want. Go tell the engineer to let us down six turns."

"That I will," said the old man. "It's my son what's down there."

"We'll have him up by to-morrow or next day."

"I hope to God ye will. Like as though he'd starve atween whiles."

5

"I've thought of that, and I mean to send food to him as soon as possible."

"The like o' that will not be easy. But ye be a boss miner—I can see that."

Breewood joined the carpenters on the trolley, and just as they started down he addressed the crowd of people that swarmed about the pit's mouth, and said that the lost men would undoubtedly be recovered, but probably not for several hours. They had better disperse and wait quietly at home. But the people would do nothing of the kind. Some few returned to the town below, but it was only to bring up food to those who remained.

The trolley slid quickly down the slope, and the crew were soon in the dim light from the oil-lamps on their caps. Suddenly the trolley stopped. Breewood sprang out upon the steep road-way with the stone hammer in hand, and struck three hard blows on the back wall of coal that formed that side of the slope. They listened intently, but there was nothing, save the appalling silence of the mine, the dead, lifeless silence of the earth one hundred and seventy feet below the sod. Then he knocked again three times, and they listened in breathless attention. Were the men already lost in the darkness and the rising flood? At last there were knockings,—faint, indistinct, confused; a strange call for help through fifteen hundred feet of solid coal. The men were still alive, imprisoned by the water at the top of some slope.

"Seems as if they were telegraphing," said one of the carpenters. "That Dennis Nagle worked in the telegraph office at one time."

"You're right. It's Morse's alphabet he is using. We must have the operator down here and then we can speak to them. Now, men, rig up a platform here for the steam-pumps. Make it the whole size of the slope and very strong."

The men sprang to the work quickly. It was a case of life and death, a rescue from the rising flood in the mine. The moment the trolley was unloaded, Breewood pulled the signal rope and went up the slope, leaving the men to make the platform. At the pit's mouth the people stood ten deep, eager and anxious to hear news from the imprisoned men below. Breewood called for volunteers, and at once selected six bosses and bade them make up gangs of men to work in relays of four hours each. While the bosses were selecting the men, Breewood went to the engine-house and called the blacksmith and master-mechanic.

"We must have a drill eight hundred feet long," he said, and then, with a pencil on a board, he sketched out full working plans of an original piece of engineering construction. He also made rough plans for two wooden air-locks of novel construction. All this work took more than an hour, and in the meantime the news of the disaster had spread over the country

A messenger had been sent to Emberton City for a telegraph operator, and in a short time a young girl was announced as the only operator within reach. Though only a child, she bravely consented to go down the pit.

A reporter of the " New York Herald " also appeared and began voluble questions concerning the disaster and possible rescue. Breewood shut him up with decisive vigor.

" Lives depend on our work. We cannot be disturbed. You shall have every chance to see, but you must not talk to the men."

The reporter retired within himself and considered the matter :

" A Great Disaster.

Three men buried alive.

Science to the rescue.

Splendid technical ability aiding Humanity."

That was the way he put it in " displayed capitals " in his own mind.

" I'm not a scientific man, but I can observe and I can dig."

With that he rushed off and telegraphed for help, —a scientific writer,—and twenty minutes after, a booky fellow from the home office was crossing the Jersey Central ferry bound for Emberton City.

Twenty-five minutes later a dozen men were laying a wire on impromptu poles up the mountain to the pit's mouth. Thirty minutes later, one of the men on Jimmy Brown's gang had sold out his place, his pick and his mining suit and lamp to the reporter for seventy-five dollars.

The trolley rolled up to the edge of the slope, and this time it held Breewood, Jimmy Brown and his gang, and a young girl—the telegraph operator. It went down amid a rousing cheer from a thousand throats and was lost in the darkness of the pit.

The trolley stopped at the platform and they all got out. The platform was finished and even boarded over.

"Now, my girl, you must help us. I'll knock on the wall, and you must listen and see what you can make out."

The girl was trembling and a trifle frightened at the semi-darkness, the awful silence, and the strange glare falling on black faces about her. Breewood took her hand in his and offered her a seat on a plank, and then with the other hand he struck three blows on the wall. The men stood round in solemn silence, listening and wondering what the "new boss" meant.

Again the knockings, so faint and far away that it was almost impossible to distinguish any sound at all! The girl leaned against Breewood and trembled with an undefinable fear. Her lips were parted, and she stared with wide eyes at the lamp on Breewood's cap. Suddenly she sighed.

"Oh! I—I hear them. They say—they—they are calling! 'Help! help! Attention! attention! help——'"

Then she suddenly dropped her head and fainted away.

"This will never do," said Breewood. "Any man got any liquor?"

"I have," said one of the men, pulling out a brandy-flask. Breewood looked at the man sharply, and some of the others laughed, but no comment was made, though the reporter had most foolishly shown himself. Breewood took the flask and forced the girl to swallow some of the liquor, and the carpenters offered some water in a tin mug. By a little effort they revived her.

"You must not be frightened, my child. You're perfectly safe."

"Yes, sir. But the men in there! It is horrible."

"So it is, and everything depends on you. You can help us save them. See! we can tap on the wall and talk to them."

Breewood made a motion as if striking the wall of coal with the stone-hammer.

"Give me the hammer and I'll speak to them."

The men instinctively broke into a cheer, and

the girl smiled, blushed, and bravely stood up and began pounding on the wall. Then she paused and listened, and instantly came the faint, murmurous knockings. The girl did not speak, and in a moment she began to strike the coal again, in curious strokes, long and short. Then the far-away sounds began again and continued for some time, while the girl stood with her ear at the wall, listening intently.

"They say they are caught at the top of the third slope. There are three of them. The water has shut them in and——"

The knockings began again, and in a moment the girl said :

"They want the inclination."

"They want the pitch of the slope, the new drift, so as to work toward us," said Jimmy Brown, the gang boss. "It will be a fall of nearly one in ten, I reckon."

Breewood bade the girl send word that they would cut them out as soon as possible, and would descend about ten feet in a hundred. The exact pitch would be given as soon as possible.

"Now, men, to work ! Drive a heading about three feet wide and five high."

"That's too big," said Jimmy Brown. "We'll be a week getting through."

"No, because the spoil must be passed up from hand to hand."

" Aye, ye be right. Come, lads! To the rescue !"

Two of the men raised their picks to strike, and the instant after the coal was spattering about on the platform floor. One of the carpenters raised a plank to make a hole to throw the spoil down the slope, for there would be no time to raise it by the trolley, and the others, with Breewood and the girl, got on board the trolley, and were quickly drawn up to daylight.

As Breewood stepped off the trolley, he was met by the superintendent, furious and insolent. What right had the clerk to order men and materials about in this extraordinary manner ?

" The accident threw every thing into confusion, and I took charge of the people, and made preparations to rescue the men below. I will show you my plans and surrender the work to you."

The man doubted if any men were left alive, and preferred to carry out his own plans.

" There are three men caught at the top of the third slope. We heard from them and sent word to them."

The superintendent laughed. Hear from men through fifteen hundred feet of coal ! Impossible !

Breewood made neither resistance nor remonstrance to the superintendent's power, and merely explained his plans for the rescue.

" Yes, and supposing your machine works,—and

it will not,—the moment you reach the men the air will escape, and the water will rise and drown them."

" Air-locks are provided," said Breewood, and before he could add more, a gentleman, who had joined the crowd of people who had gathered near, said quickly :

" Mr. Superintendent, you will place this young man in charge of the rescue party, and give him every aid in your power."

It was the president of the coal company, who, hearing of the disaster, had come up on a special engine from Pottsville.

Three minutes later, a messenger was dispatched for surveying instruments ; the company's engine and a powerful freight-locomotive were brought up the tracks as near the pit as possible. Machinists were put to work upon them to make steam connections with them up the mountain-side, so that they could be used to provide steam for the pumps. The mayor was sent for to call out a police force to keep away the surging mass of people who swarmed about the breaker and pit. Breewood personally laid out the new rescue drift, and, in the presence of the president, showed how the girl operator could telegraph by sound through the coal to the men locked up at the head of Slope No. 3.

By sundown all the work was well under way,

5*

and over a hundred men were busy at the immense task laid out by the engineer. The steam-pumps and the pipe arrived from Pottsville and were put in position at the platform and properly connected with the two locomotives. By this device two extra boilers had been obtained, and by nine o'clock in the evening two enormous streams of water were pouring from four-inch pipes and rushing in a brook down the mountain-side. The miners, with wedge, pick, and hammer, made vigorous progress at the new drift running down through the coal. Men were stationed at short intervals along the drift to pass up the baskets of loose coal and throw it down the hole left in the platform.

Very soon the heat of the steam-pumps and the confined air of the drift became unbearable. Ventilation must be provided or the work would come to a stop.

Breewood was thinking of this as he stood at the pit's mouth, listening to the rush of water thrown up by the steam-pumps. Suddenly, he pushed through the crowd and ran back to the shop, where the men were at work on his new drill. Picking up a piece of four-inch pipe, he chalked a mark for a hole to be drilled in the side, and set a man at the work. To another man he gave a piece of two-inch pipe, with directions to cut it up into lengths, and to join these with elbows according to a pattern that he hastily drew on a board. In an hour he had four injectors, formed of iron pipes one within the other, the larger designed for steam, the smaller for air. These he had secured to the exhaust pipes of the steam pumps and the hoisting engine. There were four exhausts in all, and he thus had four steam injectors, on the principle of the vacuum brake, and each connected by branch pipes with a two-inch pipe laid down the slope and into the new cut. Within an hour, the new injectors were at work sucking the foul, heated air from the pit, and throwing it out with the steam, with a dull, roaring sound.

A late and waning moon rose on this scene of intense activity, and thousands of people sat up to hear the news from the pit. Hundreds of men, wrapped in thick cloaks, lined the high-level bridge of the breaker, and watched the firemen firing the two locomotives and listened to the incessant hammering in the machine-shop, and the deep, booming roar of the great steam-injectors. Over all flashed and flared an enormous bonfire, that had been lighted to aid the men at their work. A tent, not far away, was lighted up, and through the open door could be seen two men writing on an overturned barrel, and dispatching full descriptions of all these scenes to the " Herald."

It was nearly morning as Breewood came out on the high bridge of the breaker and gazed down on the men busy about the two locomotives doing strange duty on the tracks below. He looked abroad over the mountains, the sleeping town, and the strange, wild scene, and wondered if it was not all a dream to melt away in the morning. Some one drew near.

"Young man, you must have rest. This sort of work is wearing on you. Everything is going on well now, and you must go home and sleep. I will take charge of the work while you rest."

After some urging, Breewood consented to the president's request, and went down the long stairs of the breaker and on down the mountain-side to the deserted town. Here and there were lights, as if some still watched for those lost in the deeper darkness underground and for the heroic souls who toiled to rescue them.

At his own home he found a light burning and a supper laid for him. He ate a little, and then threw himself upon the sofa and instantly fell asleep.

At ten o'clock he awoke to what seemed a new and fairer day. There was a fire burning brightly in the room, and on the table was an inviting breakfast. Maria sat by the fire, as if watching for him to awake. He looked at her for a moment, and recognized her kind attention to his comfort.

"You are very kind, Maria."

She was startled, and rose and came toward him with a bright blush upon her face.

" Oh ! I am very glad you have waked. Breakfast is ready. Do you feel rested ? I thought you
would like a fire, and—I didn't mean to stay here
so long."

" It is of no consequence. I am glad to have
your company."

She drew nearer, and he observed a tremulous
brightness in her eyes, a half-smiling eagerness to
add to his comfort, mingled with an earnest solici-
tude, but ill-suppressed. For whom could she show
so much feeling ? He could but think she loved
him. He had thought once, in a general way,
of the reception this buxom mountain maiden
would meet in the thin air of the Brahmin quarter
of Boston. But all doubt or fear on this score was
swept away now. He believed she loved him, and
he felt sure he could love so fine a specimen of vigorous womanhood.

Immediately after breakfast, Breewood went to his
room and in high glee prepared for his day's work.
Now he could work, indeed, helped and applauded
by such a splendid creature. When he came back,
ready to go to the mine, Maria also appeared
dressed as if to go out. Would she like to go to the
mine ? Oh! gladly, if he would take her. So
they set out together. At the door she took his
arm, as he thought, by a natural impulse, and they
thus walked through the streets till they came to
the open fields outside the town.

It seemed as if all the country side had met upon the mountain. Hundreds of carriages and country wagons were tethered to the fences. An excursion train was discharging a multitude of people, and thousands of men, women, and children swarmed over the rough, bare mountain, treading the snow into black mud. The coal-breaker was crowded with men, and there were several tents on the slope near the engine-house. There was also a gleam of bayonets, for the militia had been called out to keep the crowd away from the works. Our hero pressed eagerly forward, and his companion, quite as eagerly, kept pace with him. At the breaker they came to the two locomotives still busy at their new work ; but here there was a delay, for the guard would allow no one to pass. Then the men on the engines saw them, and there was a cheer for "the new boss," and the guard gave way, but objected to Miss Baumgarten.

"My friend must go with me," said Breewood.

"Oh, that's all right!" was the significant answer, and they both passed on.

At the pit's mouth they met the president of the company, and Maria was introduced by Breewood as "my friend." The president smiled graciously, but made no comment, and immediately called attention to the progress of the work. The new drift had advanced three hundred and five feet, but the water was steadily rising in spite of the pumps.

Breewood said he would go down the pit at once, and the trolley was signalled and brought up. The telegraph operator came up on it with the men, and they reported that she had heard from the men below, who had appealed for speedy help, saying that they could not hold out much longer.

" Oh ! " cried Maria, " it is dreadful to think of them buried alive and in darkness and without food."

" We shall send them food by to-night or to-morrow morning," said Breewood.

" Oh ! I hope so, indeed."

Had Breewood been less interested in the work before him, he would have noticed the tears that had gathered in her eyes, but he did not see them and at once set out for the pit below. Maria drew back at first and then suddenly requested to be taken also. To this he would not consent, and Maria pouted and began to cry in dead earnest. Breewood was vexed, but said nothing, and they parted, he going down the pit and she returning home.

It was a great and notable day in the young man's life. He was the hero and master of the hour. By three o'clock the new drill was finished, and by night the rescue drift had advanced five hundred and thirty-four feet, a decided gain on the first day. So much for a re-enforcement of one man. The men who toiled in the dark and narrow heading, worked with twice the energy when directed by the young engineer.

Still he could not keep away from the town, and he went back regularly to his meals. Maria was all attention, yet, with it all, was a certain tearful anxiety that evidently came from his refusal to take her down the pit. He asked her pardon, and she smiled and said it was of no consequence. He now felt sure that he truly loved her. How could he help it, when she so plainly loved him? Besides, was not his rising fame, now flown over the whole land, sure to win him a home that would be worthy of her?

By midnight the drift had advanced 709 feet from the slope and downward seventy-one feet, as the drift was sunk on an incline of ten feet in 100. Work was then stopped for the purpose of drilling through the remaining 790 feet to the imprisoned men, in order that food might be sent to them.

The problem was to drill a small hole through the coal to the men below, that food might be sent down to them. The men were caught at the top of a sloping gallery, closed at the bottom by the water, the top of the gallery being below its level, and the water being prevented from rising in the slope by the air imprisoned with them. If now an opening was made through the coal, the air would escape and the water would rise and submerge the gallery, and even drown out the rescue party, for they also were below the water-level. No ordinary tool could reach the men, and Breewood had designed and constructed of such materials as were at hand a rock drill for the purpose. Two switch-frames from the railroad were set up in the drift as a support for a long shaft, carrying a hand-crank and a geared wheel. The gear fitted into another gear on a second shaft, and this shaft turned the rock-drill. A feeding appliance was rigged up behind the machine to enable the man who tended the apparatus to force or " feed" the tool up to its work. At the end of the drill was the cutting-head, designed to break and crush its way through the coal. To allow for the advance of the drill the driving wheel was keyed to its shaft by a long key. The cutter-head was made of wrought-iron pipe having teeth cut in the end and case-hardened, the teeth being " set " alternately outward and inward, so as to crush the coal as it advanced. This was screwed to the end of a pipe that could be lengthened as the drill progressed, and the combined apparatus made a powerful and efficient boring tool.

The machine was taken in parts into the pit and down to the end of the drift, and was there set up with the cutter-head against the coal. A man was stationed at the crank and another behind, where a timber had been braced against the feed-motion appliance, and with a bar in his hand ready to . " feed " or push the drill up to its work.

The men stood ready, silent and grim in the murky darkness. The air pipe on the floor whistled as it sucked up the air, and there was a pause. At the word from the president, the big fellow turned the crank and the cutter-head began to crush and grind into the coal, tearing and rending its way downward upon its noble errand.

It was terrible work on the men, breaking them down in about fifteen minutes; but as one failed another sprang to his place in an instant. The "Herald" reporter gave out in about four minutes, but that did not hinder him from taking full and careful notes of all that happened. Breewood timed the tool and found that it was moving into the coal at the rate of ninety feet an hour. At that rate it would get through in about eight hours.

To record every rtep of this remarkable rescue would fill a book. There was toil, trouble, delay, and it was mose than twelve hours before the drill came within twenty feet of the imprisoned men. Breewood was asleep at the time, and a messenger came in hot haste to the house. Maria, who met the man at the door, was all eagerness and joy to hear that the drill had nearly reached the imprisoned men. She would call Mr. Breewood at once.

When Breewood reached the end of the steep, dark gallery where the men were at work, he found a new danger threatening both the lost men and the rescuing party. The two steam-pumps were lifting

15,000 gallons of water an hour, and still the water had gained on them. It had risen in the slope to within twenty feet of the platform, and was, therefore, over the heads of the rescue party below. The pressure would be enormous, and they must guard against an explosion of air when the drill broke through into the cave where the lost men were imprisoned.

The last length of pipe had a small branch pipe at the side, and on this was secured a pressure-gauge to indicate the pressure of the air in, the slope below when the tool passed through. Besides this it had two air-locks or gates to prevent the escape of the air through the drill.

Suddenly the man at the crank fell forward, and the handle slipped out of his hand.

The drill was through! It turned freely in the coal, and the pressure-gauge marked a pressure of five pounds per square inch. The men had been reached, and if they were still alive, food could be sent to them. While the drill was moving, it made so much noise that the knocking could not be heard. For a moment there was a solemn silence in the dark and narrow hole in which these heroes worked. Then came a tapping on the pipe. They were alive! They had found the drill!

Breewood went up to the daylight to get the carriers and food, and was surprised to find Maria waiting with soup, bread, and meat for the men.

A tin carriage on wheels was loaded with food and inserted in the drill, and one air-lock was opened when it rolled down to the second. The lock behind was closed and the second opened, and then they heard it roll away down to the men below.

A mighty cheer went up from the people who still lingered in multitudes about the pit when the news was sent up that the drill had reached the men. Within two hours, posters were up in every city, from Boston to Chicago, announcing the fact. Extras were published every few hours in all the large cities, and the progress of the rescue was noted by millions of readers.

The discovery of the great pressure under which the men were confined alarmed the president and the mining engineers and experts who had gathered from far and near, and doubts were expressed as to the possibility of bringing up the men alive. Everybody said they would be lost the moment the pick struck through their prison wall, should the air be released. The rescuers, also, would be exposed to instant death, as they, too, were below the level of the rising water in the mine.

Breewood had but one reply—air-locks ! These he had wisely ordered in advance, and when the work was resumed, as soon as the prisoners below had been fed, one of these locks was put in place. A deep slot was cut in the coal all round the rescue drift, and in this was set a stout door-frame.

All the cracks were filled with cement, and an airtight door was hinged to the frame. Five feet lower down a second door was put up in the same manner.

So the hours went on. The relays of men were changed rapidly, and pick and shovel were worked with all the energy of despair. The water was now within ten feet of the platform. Another pump, throwing ten thousand gallons an hour, came up from Philadelphia and was set to work. Still the water crept higher and higher. Breewood seldom went up to daylight; his meals were sent down to him. Once when he went up, about midnight, he found Maria sitting watchful in the engine-room among the anxious company of officers, engineers, miners, soldiers, and reporters, who were waiting for news. There were other women also waiting for news, but they had sons or husbands below. She waited for him and he was glad.

The hours slipped swiftly away. It was day again and then night. The water had gained four more feet in spite of the three enormous pumps pouring a muddy torrent down the mountain-side.

At last word came up. Only ten feet more! A last call for volunteers! This time there was death and danger to be faced. The working party were to be locked in behind the air-locks when they broke through the wall!

There were six miners,—all unmarried men (to

save making widows),—Breewood, old Josh Binny, the boss, and the reporter. The president shook Breewood by the hand at the first air-lock, and with his own hands barred them in. It was a moment of intense suspense. The Catholic church bell rang for midnight prayers for their safety. The entire population stood in the streets or on the mountain-side in anxious silence.

With a splintering crash Josh Binny's pick went through, making a hole like a man's hand. Then came a silence. Were they all dead? There was a slight rush of air, and the rescuers stood in breathless suspense. Then came a feeble cheer through the hole. They were alive! To break out the hole, to drag the men, half dead, through the opening, to carry them up the drift past the second air-lock, took just twenty minutes. Then Breewood closed the wooden air-lock. They were still all under the pressure of the imprisoned air, and under water. Would the air-lock hold while they escaped into the slope?

.   .   .   .

Slowly the trolley crept up the slope burdened with the saved and savers. Breewood stood erect on the front of the trolley, his face shining with joy and triumph. His love should see his day of success, should share in his honors. The trolley rose to daylight in the centre of an immense throng of people, for it was day once more.

At sight of the rescued men lying pale and feeble on the floor of the trolley, the crowd broke into
a shout of joy and triumph. It echoed down the
mountain-side, and the people shouted in hoarse
hurrahs. Every whistle screamed, and all the
church bells rang in sonorous chorus. Here were
honors indeed for the young engineer. Every wire
in the country was telling his fame to the people.

Suddenly, a woman burst through the crowd of
people about the trolley and fell upon one of the
prostrate men with a cry of joy, covering his face
with kisses and passionate tears. It was Maria,
welcoming her rescued lover—John Krumburger.

APPLIED SCIENCE: A LOVE STORY.

THE village of Salmon Falls, in eastern New England, consists of a number of mills and factories, the railroad station, a store or two, and two hundred dwellings. Among these is the Denny mansion at the top of the hill, where the road climbs up from the station and the river. It is a large square house in the old colonial fashion, with two wings at the rear and a garden in front.

It was a warm July morning when Mr. John Denny, mill-owner and proprietor of the homestead, had his chair rolled out to the porch, and with some assistance from the servants, reached it on his crutch and sat down in the shadow of the great house and out of the glare of the hot sun. The vine-covered porch and the wide piazza opened directly upon the garden and gave a full view of the road. Beyond there was an outlook over the open fields, the mills, the stream, and the village in the valley. By the road there was a stone wall and a wicker gate opening upon the grassy sidewalk outside. A table had been laid with a white cloth in the porch, and Mr. Denny sat by·it and waited for the coming of his daughter and breakfast. While he sat thus he turned over a number of papers, and then, after a while, he began to talk to himself somewhat in this wise :

"Expense! expense! expense! There seems no end to it. Bills coming in every day, and every one larger than was expected. In my young days we built a shop and knew to a dollar what it would cost. Now the estimates are invariably short. The batting mill has already gone a thousand dollars beyond the estimates, and the roof is but just put on. Even the new chimney cost four dollars a foot more than was expected. Thank Heaven it is done, and that expense is over. Could I walk, I might look after things and keep them within bounds. With my crushed foot I sit a prisoner at home, and must leave all to Lawrence. It is fortunate that I have one man I can trust with my affairs."

Just here Alma, his only child, a bright and wholesome girl of nineteen, appeared from the house. Fairly educated, sensible, and affectionate, but perhaps a trifle inexperienced by reason of her residence in this quiet place, she is at once the pride and the light of the house.

"Good-morning, father. Are you well this happy summer's day ? "

6

The old gentleman kissed her fondly, and asked did she pass a quiet night.

" Oh, yes.   I didn't sleep much, that is all—for thinking."

" Thinking of what ? "

" The expected guest.   To-day is the 9th of July, and cousin Elmer comes."

" Ah, yes—Elmer Franklin.   I had almost forgotten him."

" How does he look, father?   Is his hair dark, or has he blue eyes ?   I hardly know which I like best."

" I do not remember.   I've not seen the boy since he was a mere child, years ago.   He has been at school since."

" He must be a man now.   He is past twenty-one, and, as for school, why, it's the Scientific School, and I'm sure men go to that."

" You seem greatly interested in this unknown relative, Alma."

" He is to be our guest, father—for a whole month.   Come !   Will you have breakfast out here in the porch ? "

" Yes, dear.   It is quite comfortable here, and it will save the trouble of moving."

Thereupon Alma entered the house in search of the breakfast, and a moment after Mr. Lawrence Belford entered the garden at the street gate. The son of an old friend of Mr. Denny's lamented wife, Mr. Belford had been admitted to the house some months since as confidential clerk and business man. He was a rather commonplace person, about thirty years of age, and his education and manners were good if not remarkable. During his residence with the Dennys he had found time to fall in love with Alma, and they had been engaged—and with Mr. Denny's consent.

" Good-morning, Lawrence. You're just in time for breakfast."

" Good-morning, sir. Thank you, no. I have been to breakfast. I am just up from the station."

" Seen anything of the railroad coach ? The train is in, and it is time for the coach to pass. Our guest may be in it."

" No, sir, but I saw the express coming up the hill with an extra large load of baggage."

Just here Alma returned from the house bearing a large tray of plates and breakfast things. The young people greet each other pleasantly, and Alma proceeds to lay the table.

" Now for breakfast, father. Everything waits upon a good appetite. Will you not join us, Lawrence ? "

Mr. Belford replies that he has been to breakfast. Mr. Denny takes a cup of coffee, and while sipping it remarks :

" How many more window-frames shall you require for the new mill, Lawrence ? "

"Ten more, sir. There is only a part of the fourth story unfinished."

"Alma, dear, do you remember how high we decided the new chimney was to be ? Yes, thank you, only two lumps of sugar. Thank you. You remember we were talking about it when the Lawsons were here."

"Don't ask me. Ask Lawrence. I never can remember anything about such matters."

Just at that moment the express pulled up at the gate, and there was a knock. Alma rose hastily, and said :

"Oh ! That must be Elmer."

She opened the gate, and young Mr. Elmer Franklin of New York entered. A man to respect : an open, manly face, clear blue eyes, and a wiry, compact, and vigorous frame. A man with a sound mind in a sound body. He was dressed in a gray travelling suit, and had a knapsack strapped to his back ; in his hand a stout stick looking as if just cut from the roadside, and at his side a field glass in a leather case. Immediately behind him came a man bending under the load of an immense trunk. Alma smiled her sweetest, and the young stranger bowed gallantly.

"Mr. Denny, I presume ? "

"Welcome, cousin Franklin," said Mr. Denny from his chair. "I knew you at once, though it is years since any members of our families have met. Pardon me if I do not rise. I'm an old man, and confined to my chair."

Mr. Franklin offered his hand and said politely :

"Thank you, sir, for your kind reception. I am greatly pleased to——Hullo ! Look out there, boys ! That baggage is precious and fragile."

Another man appeared, and the two brought in trunks and boxes, bundles and parcels, till there was quite a large heap of baggage piled up on the grass. Alma and Lawrence were properly amazed at this array of things portable, and Mr. Denny laid aside the breakfast things to look at the rather remarkable display.

The young man seemed to think apologies essential.

"I do not wonder that you are alarmed. I do not often take such a load of traps. I wrote you that my visit would be one of study and scientific investigation, and I was obliged to bring my philosophical apparatus and books with me."

"It is indeed a wonderful train of luggage for a man. One would have thought you intended to bring a wife."

Then Mr. Denny bethought him of his duty, and he introduced his newly found relative to his daughter and to Mr. Lawrence Belford, and then bade him draw up to the table for breakfast. The young man made the motions suitable for such an occasion, and then he turned to pay his express-

man. This trifling incident deserves record as
happily illustrating the young man's noble character.

"Thank you, sir. Breakfast will be a cheerful
episode. I've a glorious appetite, for I walked up
from the station."

"There's a coach, Mr. Franklin, and it passes
our door."

"I knew that, sir, but I preferred to walk and
see the country. Fine section of conglomerate
you have in the road cutting just above the station."

"Eh! What were you saying?"

"I said that I observed an interesting section of
conglomerate—water-worn pebbles, I should say
—mingled with quartz sand, on the roadside. I
must have a run down there and a better look at it
after breakfast."

Mr. Denny was somewhat overwhelmed at this,
and said doubtfully:

"Ah, yes, I remember—yes, exactly."

"Are you interested in geology, Miss Denny?"

Alma was rather confused, and tried hard to find
the lump of sugar that had melted away in her
coffee, and said briefly:

"No. I didn't know that we had any in this
part of the country."

Mr. Belford here felt called upon to say:

"My dear Alma, you forget yourself."

" Why will you take me up so sharply, Law-rence? I meant to say that I didn't know we had any quartz conglomerate hereabouts."

Mr. Franklin smiled pleasantly, and remarked to himself:

" My dear Alma! That's significant. Wonder if he's engaged to her? "

Then he said aloud :

" The pursuit of science demands good dinners. Pardon me if I take some more coffee."

" Yes, do—and these rolls. I made them my-self—expressly for you."

" Thank you for both rolls and compliment."

Mr. Lawrence took up some of the papers from the table and began to read them, and the others went on with their breakfast. Presently Mr. Denny said :

" I presume, Mr. Franklin, that you are greatly interested in your school studies ? "

" Yes, sir. The pursuit of pure science is one of the most noble employments that can tax the cultivated intellect."

" But you must confess that it is not very practi-cal."

Before the young man could reply Alma spoke :

" Oh ! cousin Elmer—I mean Mr. Franklin—ex-cuse me. You haven't taken off your knapsack."

Taking it off and throwing it behind him on the ground, he said :

"It's only my clothes."

"Clothes!" said Mr. Denny. "Then what is in the trunks?"

"My theodolite, cameras, chains, levels, telescopes, retorts, and no end of scientific traps."

Alma, quite pleased:

"How interesting. Won't you open one of the trunks and let us see some of the things?"

"With the greatest pleasure; but perhaps I'd better take them to my room first."

"Anything you like, Elmer—Mr. Franklin, I mean. Our house is your home."

Lawrence Belford here frowned and looked in an unpleasant manner for a moment at the young stranger, who felt rather uncomfortable, though he could scarcely say why. With apparent indifference he drew out a small brass sounder, such as is used in telegraph offices, and began snapping it in his fingers.

In his mind he said:

"Wonder if any of them are familiar with the great dot and line alphabet!"

Alma heard the sounder and said eagerly:

"Oh! Mr. Franklin, what is that?"

"It is a pocket sounder. Do you know the alphabet?"

"I should hope so."

"I beg pardon. I meant Morse's."

"Morse's?"

" Yes. Morse's alphabet."

" No. You must teach it to me."

Thereupon he moved the sounder slowly, giving a letter at a time, and saying :

" A - — L- — - · M — — A - —. That's your name. Queer sound, isn't it ? "

" Let me try. Perhaps I could do it."

" My dear Alma, your father is waiting. You had best remove the things."

" Yes, Lawrence. I'll call Mary."

The maid soon appeared, and the breakfast things were removed. Then Mr. Denny drew Mr. Franklin's attention to the new factory chimney that stood in plain sight from where they sat.

The young man promptly drew out his field glass, and, mounting one of the steps of the porch, took a long look at the new shaft.

" Not quite plumb, is it ? "

" Not plumb ! What do you mean ? "

" It is impossible," said Mr. Belford with some warmth.

" It looks so," said the young man with the glass still up at his eyes.

" I tell you it is impossible, sir. I built it myself, and I ought to know."

" Oh ! Beg pardon. You can take the glass and see for yourself."

" I need no glass. I took the stage down only yesterday, and I ought to know."

6*

"Allow me to take your glass, cousin Franklin," said Mr. Denny. He took the glass, but quickly laid it down with a sigh.

"My eyes are old and weak, and the glass does not suit them. I am very sorry to hear what you say. I would not have one of my chimneys out of line for the world."

"I am sorry I said anything about it, sir. I did not know the chimney belonged to you."

Alma was apparently distressed at the turn the conversation had taken, and tried to lead it to other matters, but the old gentleman's mind was disturbed, and he returned to the chimney.

"I designed it to be the tallest and finest chimney I ever erected, and I hope it is all correct."

"It is, sir," said Mr. Belford. "Everything is correct to the very capstones."

"It is my tallest chimney, Mr. Franklin—eighty-one feet and six inches; and that is two feet taller than any chimney in the whole Salmon Falls valley."

Mr. Franklin, in an innocent spirit of scientific inquiry, put his glass to his eyes and examined the chimney again. Alma began to feel ill at ease, and Lawrence Belford indulged in a muttered curse under his black moustache.

"Eighty-one feet and six inches—the tallest chimney in the valley."

No one seemed to heed the old gentleman's remark, and presently Mr. Franklin laid his field glass on the table, and taking out his brass sounder, he idly moved it as if absently thinking of some-thing.

Alma suddenly looked up with a little blush and a smile. Her eyes seemed to say to him :

" I heard you call ? What is it ? "

He nodded pleasantly, and said, " Would you like to see some of my traps ? "

" Oh, yes. Do open one of your trunks."

Mr. Franklin took out a bunch of keys and went to one of the trunks. As he did so he said to him-self :

" Deuced bright girl ! She learned my call in a flash. I must teach her the whole alphabet, and then we'll have some tall fun and circumvent that fool of a clerk."

This remark was applied to Mr. Belford, and was afterward eminent for its truthfulness.

While the young people were opening the trunk, Mr. Denny and Mr. Belford were engaged in ex-amining the business papers spread on the table, and for several minutes they paid no attention to things done and said almost under their eyes.

Such a very strange trunk. Instead of clothing, it contained the most singular assortment of scien-tific instruments. Each was carefully secured so that no rude handling would harm it, and all shin-ing and glistening brilliantly as if kept with the

most exquisite care. Mr. Franklin unfastened a
small brass telescope, mounted upon a stand, with
a compass, levels, plumb line, and weight attached.

"That's my theodolite.   There's a tripod in one
of my boxes.   I'll get it and mount it, and we'll
have a shot at the chimney."

"What do you mean ? "

"Oh, nothing !   I'm going to measure it.
Wouldn't you like to help me ? "

"With all my heart.   Tell me what to do."

"Presently.   Wait till I've screwed things together ; then I'll tell you what to do.   Oh ! By the
way, I must tell you an amusing episode that happened at the railroad station while I was waiting for
my luggage.   There was a young man sending off
a message at the little telegraph station, and I over-
heard the message and the comments of the operator."

Alma didn't appear to enjoy this incident.

"Not listening intentionally, you know.   It was
the telegraph I heard, not the people."

Alma felt better.

"It was all by mere sounds, and it ran this way :
'The old fool is here again.'   That's what she said
—the operator, I mean.   'To Isaac Abrams, 1,607
Barclay street, New York.   I have secured the will.
Foreclose the mortgage and realize at once.   Get
two state rooms for the 25th.—L. B.'   That was the
message, and it was so very strange I wrote it out

in my—— Oh! Beg pardon, Miss Denny. Are you ill?"

Alma's face had assumed a sudden pallor, and she seemed frightened and ill at ease.

" 'Tis nothing—really nothing! I shall be better presently."

Then, as if anxious to change the conversation, she began to ask questions about the theodolite and its uses.

Mr. Franklin was too well bred to notice anything, but he confessed to himself that he had said something awkward, and, for the life of him, he could not imagine what it might be. He replied briefly, and then went on with his preparations for some time in silence, Alma meanwhile looking on with the greatest interest. The theodolite having been put together, Mr. Franklin opened another box and took out a wooden tripod, such as are used to support such instruments. He also took out a fine steel ribbon, or measuring tape, neatly wound up on a reel.

"You shall carry that, Miss Denny, and I'll shoulder the theodolite."

"Wait till I get my hat and the sun umbrella."

"To be sure; it will be warm in the fields."

Alma was soon arrayed in a dainty chip. At least she called it a chip, and the historian can do naught but repeat her language. Besides this, it was not bigger than a chip, and it looked very pretty tied under her chin. ·Over her head she carried its real protection, an immense Japanese paper umbrella, light, airy, and generous.

"Where are you going, Alma?" said Mr. Denny.

"Oh! only to the fields for a little walk. We'll be back presently."

The confidential clerk thought it strange that the daughter of the house should be so free with the stranger. But the young people were distant cousins, and it wouldn't have been polite in him to have objected to the little walk.

So the two, under the friendly shade of the big paper umbrella, went out to see the new chimney, while Mr. Denny and the confidential clerk stayed behind to talk business.

The new chimney stood at the southeast corner of the great four-story mill, and close beside the little brick engine house. Alma led the youthful son of science out of the gate, down the road a few rods, and then they passed a stile, and took the winding path that straggled over the pastures to the mill.

Of course they talked volubly. This being the stern and prosy record of applied science, it be-·comes us not to report the chatterings of these two till they reached the base of the vast brick chimney, towering nearly eighty feet into the air above them. Its long shadow lay like a stiffened snake upon the fields, and Elmer, observing it, said :

" Good ! We can use the shadow, too, and have double proof."

" How ? " said the bright one, in a beautiful spirit of inquiry.

" If an upright stick, a foot long, casts a shadow three feet long, the shadow of another stick beside it, at the same time, is proportionally long."

" I knew that before. That isn't very high science."

" Why did you say ' how ' ? "

" Because I didn't think. Because I was a goose."

" Such terms are not choice, and are devoid of truth. Here! stern duty calls. Do you hold one end of the tape at the foot of the chimney, and I'll measure off the base line of our triangle."

Alma was charmed to be of use, and sat on a stone with the brass ring of the tape on her ring finger next her engagement ring, and her hand flat against the first course of bricks. Trifles sometimes hint great events. Little did she think that the plain brass ring on her finger was the hard truth of science that should shiver her gold ring to fragments and pale its sparkling diamond. Being a wholesome creature, and not given to romance, she thought nothing about it, which was wise. Her cousin, the knight of the theodolite, set his instrument upright upon the grass, and then ran the measuring line out to its full length.

"All right! Let the tape go."

Alma took off the brass ring, and the steel ribbon ran like a glittering snake through the grass, and she slowly followed it and joined her knight.

"Once more, please. · Hold the ring on this bit of a stake that I've set up in the ground."

Alma, like a good girl, did as she was bid, and the ribbon ran out again to its full length. Another stake was set up, and the theodolite was placed in position and a sight obtained at the top of the tall chimney. A little figuring in a note-book, and then the son of high science quietly remarked:

"Seventy-six feet four inches—short five feet two inches."

Just here several urchins of an inquiring turn of mind drew near and began to make infantile comments, and asked with charming freedom if it was circus.

"No!" said Alma, from under her paper tent. "No! Run away, children, run away."

It was too warm for so much exertion, and they wouldn't move.

"Oh! never mind them. They don't trouble me ; and if it amuses them, it's so much clear gain."

"They are some of the factory children, and I thought they might bother you."

"Inelegant, but thoughtful." He didn't say

so. He only thought it, which was quite as well.

During this little episode the impressive facts that all this scientific exertion had brought out concerning the chimney were lost upon Alma. It was small consequence. She knew it well enough before night.

Now for the shadow by way of proof. The theodolite, paper umbrella, and admiring crowd of children trotted severally and collectively over the grass till they reached the chimney again.

"The tape-measure, Alma. You hold the ring, and I'll unreel the line."

It was surprising how quickly these two made each other's acquaintance. By the time the long shadow was measured, a stake set up, and the two shadows compared, they seemed to have known each other for weeks. Such is the surprising effect of pure science when applied to love.

Had it come to this already? She was engaged to the confidential, the chimney-builder. His ring glittered on her finger. True—all of it!

See them sauntering slowly (the thermometer at 87 degrees) homeward under the friendly shade of an oiled paper umbrella. They are indeed good friends already. They enter the house together,. and the cheerful dinner-bell greets their ears. She folds her oiled paper tent and he sets his instrument up in a corner of the great shady hall. She leads the way to the chamber that is to be his room during his stay, and then retires to her own to prepare for the frugal noontide meal.

The exact truth records that the meal was not severely frugal. It was otherwise, and so much nicer.

The entire family were assembled, and conversation was lively, considering the weather. Near the close of the meal it grew suddenly warm. The innocent son of science, proud of his accomplishments, made a most incautious statement, and the result was peculiar.

" Oh, uncle, you were saying this morning that my science was not very practical. I tried a bit of it on your chimney this morning, and what do you think I found ? "

" I'm sure I can't tell," said Mr. Denny.

" I measured it, and it is exactly seventy-six feet, four inches high."

If he had dropped a can of nitro-glycerine under the table, the effect couldn't have been more startling. Mr. Lawrence Belford dropped his fruit-knife with a sonorous rattle, his face assumed the color of frosted cake (the frosting, to be exact), and he seemed thoroughly frightened. Mr. Denny looked surprised, and said,

" What ? "

Alma said nothing, but fished for the sugar in her strawberries and cream.

"What did you say, Mr. Franklin?"

"I said that I measured the new chimney, just for the fun of the thing, and found that it is exactly seventy-six feet, four inches high."

"It's an abominable lie."

"Lawrence!" said Alma, with an appealing glance.

"Are you sure, Mr. Franklin? Have you not made some mistake?"

"You are utterly mistaken, Mr. Franklin. I measured that chimney with a line from the top, and I know your statement is entirely incorrect."

"I hope so," said the old gentleman.

"It is so, sir," added Mr. Belford; and then, waxing bolder, he said, "How could this young person, just from school, know anything of such matters? Did he build a staging, or did he climb up the inside like a chimney-sweep?"

Young Mr. Franklin saw that he had in some innocent fashion started a most disagreeable subject. Why Mr. Denny should be so disturbed and Mr. Belford so angry was past his comprehension. At the same time Mr. Belford's language was offensive, and he replied with some spirit:

"There is no need to climb the chimney, or use a line. It is a trifling affair to ascertain the height of any building with a theodolite, as you probably know."

"I tell you, sir, it is false—utterly false. Besides, you have made some mistake in the figures. You—you—but I've no patience with such boy's play. It's only fit for school children."

"Lawrence," said Alma, "you are unkind. I'm sure we meant no harm. I helped Mr. Franklin, and I'm sure he's right; besides, we measured the chimney by its shadow, and both statements were alike.

"Oh, if you've turned against me, I've nothing more to say."

Mr. Denny meanwhile seemed lost in deep study, and he hardly heeded what was going on.

"What can that boy know about such things? I tell you, it's——"

"It seems to me, Mr. Belford, you are unnecessarily excited," said Mr. Denny. "Mr. Franklin is a much younger man than you, but he showed a knowledge of this matter, and if his figures are correct——"

"They are, sir," said Elmer warmly. "I can show you the base line, and the theodolite is still at the same angle. Alma saw me measure the base, and she can tell you its length. There are the figures in my note-book."

Mr. Denny took the note-book and examined the figuring out of this problem, and Elmer went to the hall for his instrument. He returned with the theodolite still secured at the angle at which the sight had been taken. As he laid the instrument on the dining-table, he said :

" I am very sorry, uncle, that I did anything about this matter. It was done in mere sport, and I wish I had said nothing concerning it. I would not had not Mr. Belford used the language he did."

Mr. Denny ran his eye over the figures in the book, and then, with a pained expression, he said briefly,

" Everything seems to be correct."

" Damnation! I'll break his head for him, the intermeddling fool." This language was not actually used by Mr. Belford, but he thought as much. His eyes flashed, and he clenched his fists under the table. Alma's presence alone restrained him from something more violent. He appeared calm, but inwardly he was angry. This unexpected announcement concerning the chimney he had built cast a heavy shadow over him, and his conscience awoke with a sudden smart.

Alma was greatly disturbed, and ready to cry for shame and vexation. She did not, for she felt sure this was only the beginning of a new trouble, and she well knew that heavy sorrows had already invaded the house. They needed no more.

Mr. Franklin glanced from one to another in alarm. He saw that he was treading upon uncertain ground, and he wisely held his peace. After a brief and awkward pause, Mr. Belford rose, and pleading the calls of business, went out, and the unhappy interview came to an end.

It was a strange room. Its belongings stranger still. A large square chamber, with windows on three sides and a door and a fireplace on the other. Just now the fireplace had fallen from its high estate and had become a catch-all for the wrecks of much unpacking. There was a small single bed, two chairs, and an indefinite number of tables. Impossible to say how many, for they were half obscured by numberless things scientific: microscopes, a retort, small furnace, two cameras, galvanic battery, coils of wire and rubber tubing, magic lanterns, books, photographs, and papers: on a small desk a confused pile of papers; on the walls a great number of pictures and photographs.

The very den of a student of science. Hardly room to walk among the wilderness of traps, boxes, and trunks. At the window, the young man, just dressed, and taking a view of the mill and its new chimney.

" Gad ! how mad the fellow was over my little measurement. Wonder what it all means ? The girl's in trouble, the father has a grief, and the clerk—I can make nothing of him. What matter? My duty is with my books, that I may pursue pure science. The moment things become practical I drop 'em."

Then he turned and looked out of the next window.

" Fine view of the river. I must have another try at it with the camera."

He crossed the room, and standing in the bright morning sunshine, he looked about to examine the other L that had been thrown out from the back of the main building.

" That's Alma's room, and the next is the clerk's, the chimney man. The window is open, and the place looks as dark as a cave. I've a mind to light it up."

So saying he took a small hand mirror from a table near by. Holding it in the full sunlight, he moved it slowly about till the dancing spot of reflected light fell upon the open window and leaped in upon the opposite wall of the room. . The observer with steady hand moved the spot of light about till he had probed the room, and found all it contained, which was nothing save a bed and two chairs.

" Applied science reports the man is fit for treason, spoils, and that sort of thing. He has no pictures. His room is a sleeping den. The man is a——Hallo ! Steady there ! "

The door in the room opened, and the student of applied science turned quickly away with his back to the wall beside his window. Cautiously raising the mirror, he held it near the window in such a way that in it he could see all that went on in the other room, without being himself seen.

Suddenly he saw something in the glass. Some one appeared at the window, looked out as if watching for something, and then withdrew into the bare little sleeping room. Then the figure in the mirror went to the bed and carefully turned all the clothes back. The student of science watched the mirror intently. The figure bent over the uncovered mattress and quietly opened the sacking and took something out. It sat down on the edge of the disordered bed and proceeded to examine the box or bundle, whatever it might be, that it had found in the bed.

Just here there was the sound of a distant door opening and closing. The figure crouched low on the bed, as if fearing to be seen, and waited till all was quiet again. Then it slowly opened the box or package, and took out a folded paper. The student bent over the mirror with the utmost interest. What did it mean? What would happen next? Nothing in particular happened. The figure closed the box, returned it to its hiding-place in the bed, and then crept out of the range of reflected vision.

Why should the confidential clerk hide papers in his bed? What was the nature of the documents? A strange affair, certainly, but it did not concern him, and perhaps he had better drop the subject. He turned to his books and papers, and for an hour or more was too much occupied with them to heed aught else.

Suddenly there was a brisk series of taps at his door, like this :

— - — -- - - — — - - — —

" I'm here. Come in."

Alma, the bright one entered.

" What a room ! Such disorder, Elmer."

" Yes. It is quite a comfortable den. I've un-packed everything, and—mind your steps—feel quite at home—thank you."

" I should say as much. Do look at the dust. I must have Mary up here at once."

" Madam, I never allow any female person to touch my traps. Mary may make the bed, but she must not sweep, nor dust, nor touch anything."

" Oh ! really. Then I'll go at once."

" Better not."

" Why ? "

" Because I've many things to show—— "

" Oh, Elmer ! What is that—that queer thing on the table ? May I look at it ? "

" That's my new camera."

" How stupid. I might have known that. Do you take pictures ? "

" Photos ? Yes. Will you sit ? "

" Oh, dear, no. I hate photographs. It's so disagreeable to see one's self staring with some im-

7

possible expression, and sitting in an impossible palace, with a distant landscape and drapery curtains."

"Then I'll take a view for you. Find a seat somewhere while I rig things. See those two people sitting on the little bridge that crosses the race beyond the mill? I'll photograph them without their permission."

Alma looked out of the window when Elmer had raised the curtain, but declared she couldn't see anything.

"They are very far off. Take the field-glass, and you'll see them."

Alma took the glass from the table, and looked out on the sunny landscape.

"I see what you mean, but I can't make out who they are, even with the glass. It's a man and a woman, and that's as much as I can see."

"You shall see them plain enough in a moment."

So saying, Elmer placed a long brass telescope upon a stand by the open window, and through it he examined the couple on the bridge. Meanwhile, Alma gazed around the room and examined its strange contents with the greatest interest.

The moment the focus of the glass was secured, Elmer hastily took the little camera, and adjusting a plate in it from a table-drawer, he placed it before the telescope on the table and close to the eye-hole. Then, by throwing a black cloth over his head, he looked into it, turned a screw or two, and in a moment had a negative of the distant couple.

"Aren't you almost ready?"

"In one moment, Alma. I must fix this first. I'll be right back."

So saying he took the slide from the little camera, and went out of the room into a dark closet in the entry.

Alma waited patiently for a few moments, and then she took up the field-glass, and looked out of the window. Who could they be? They seemed to be having a cosy time together; but beyond the fact that one figure was a woman she could learn nothing. She wanted to take a look through the telescope, but did not dare to move the little camera that stood before it.

" Here's the picture," said Elmer as he entered the room.

Alma took the bit of glass he offered her, but declared she couldn't see anything but a dirty spot on the glass.

"That's the negative. Let me copy it, and then I'll throw it up with the stereopticon."

He selected another bit of glass from a box, and in a few minutes had it prepared and the two put together and laid in the sun on the window-seat.

" What's in that iron box, Elmer?"

" Nitrous oxide."

" The same thing that the dentists use ? "

" Yes. Would you like to try a whiff? It's rather jolly, and will not hurt you in the least."

Elmer caught up a bit of rubber pipe, secured one end to the iron chest and inserted the other in a mouth-piece having the proper inhalation and exhalation valves.

" Put that in your mouth for a moment."

Alma, with beautiful confidence, put the tube in her mouth, and in a moment her pretty head fell back against the back of the chair in deep sleep. With wonderful speed and skill Elmer rolled a larger camera that stood in a corner out into the centre of the room, ran in a plate, adjusted the focus, and before the brief slumber passed had a negative of the sleeping one.

" Oh, how odd ! What a queer sensation to feel yourself going and going, off and off, till you don't know where you are ! "

" It is rather queer. I've often taken the gas my-self—just for fun. Now, Alma, if you will let down the curtains, and close the shutters, and make the room dark, I'll light the lantern and show you the picture."

Alma shut the blinds, drew down the curtains, and closed all the shutters save one.

" Won't it be too dark ? "

" No. It must be quite dark. You can stand

here in the middle of the room and look at that bit of bare wall between the windows. I left that space clear for a screen."

Alma eagerly took her place, and said with a laugh :

" If this is the pursuit of pure science, it is very amusing. I'd like to study science—in this way."

" Yes, it is rather interesting—— "

" Oh, Elmer, it's pitch dark."

" Never mind. Stand perfectly still and watch the wall. There—there's the spot of light. Now I'll run in the positive."

A round spot of white light fell on the unpapered wall, and then two dusky shadows slid over it, vague, obscure, and gigantic.

" There are your people. Now I'll adjust the focus. There—look."

A heavy sob startled him.

" Oh ! It's that hateful Alice Green ! "

Elmer opened the door of the lantern, and the light streamed full upon Alma. She was bathed in tears, and her shoulders, visible through her light summer dress, shook with sobs.

" What's the matter ? " .

" Nothing ! Oh, it's—nothing—let me—go—— "

With an impatient gesture she tried to brush the tears from her eyes, and then, without a word, she hastily ran out of the room.

The student of pure science was surprised beyond measure. What had happened? What new blunder had he committed? With all his deep study of things material he was ignorant of things emotional and sentimental. This exhibition of anger and grief in his pretty cousin utterly disconcerted him. He did not know what to do, nor what to think, and he stood in the glare of his lantern for a moment or two in deep thought.

Then he closed the lantern and turning round, examined the shadowy picture thrown upon the wall. It represented a young man and a young woman seated upon the wooden rail of the bridge in the open air, and in most loving embrace. His arm was about her waist, and he was looking in her face. His straw hat hid his features, but the face of the young woman was turned toward the camera that had so perfectly mirrored them both. She seemed to be a young and pretty girl in the more lowly walks of life, and her lover seemed to be a gentleman. What a pity he hadn't looked up! Who could he be? And she? Alma's remark plainly showed that she at least knew the girl, and for some reason was hotly indignant with her.

Thinking he had made trouble enough already, Elmer took one more good look at the picture, and then prepared to destroy it. Something about the young man's hat struck him as familiar. It was a panama hat, and had two ribbons wound round it in a fanciful manner that was not exactly conventional.

He silently opened a shutter, and the picture faded away. He drew up the curtains and looked out on the bridge. The young couple had disappeared. Poor innocents! They little knew how their pictures had been taken in spite of themselves, and they little knew the tragic and terrible consequences that were to flow from the stolen photograph so strangely made. Elmer took the little slide from the lantern, and was on the point of shivering it to fragments on the hearthstone, when he paused in deep thought. Was it wise to destroy it? Had he not better preserve it? Perhaps he could some day solve the mystery that hung about it, and find out the cause of Alma's grief and anger. Perhaps he might help her; and there came a softening about his heart that seemed both new and wonderfully unscientific.

Shortly after this the dinner-bell rang, and he went down to the dining-room. Alma sent word that she had a severe headache and could not appear. Mr. Belford was already there, and he looked at Mr. Franklin with an expression that made the young man uncomfortable in spite of himself. Mr. Denny was unusually thoughtful and silent, and conversation between the younger men was not particularly brilliant or entertaining. At last the dreary meal was finished. Mr. Belford rose first and went out into the hall. Mr. Franklin followed him, and saw something that quite took his breath away.

There lay the hat of the photograph, double ribbons and all. Mr. Belford quietly took it up and put it on, and it fitted him perfectly. Elmer stopped abruptly and looked at the man with the utmost interest. The confidential, the chimney-builder paid no attention, and quickly passed on out of the front door.

" E. Franklin, you have made a discovery. The pursuit of pure science never showed anything half so interesting as this. You had better raise a cloud on the subject. Oh! It's cloudy enough already!"

This to himself as he slowly went upstairs to his room. Selecting a pipe, he filled it, and finding a comfortable seat, he fired up and prepared to examine mentally the events of the day.

"It was the confidential, making love to some village beauty, supposed to be 'Green,' by name, if not by nature. Alma loves him. That's bad. Perhaps she's engaged to him. Has she a ring? Yes—saw it the other day. The affair is cloudy— and. Blessed if I don't keep that lantern-slide! It may be of use some day. Come in."

This last was in response to a knock at the door. Mr. Belford entered, panama hat with two ribbons in hand.

" Good afternoon, Mr. Franklin. I thought I might find you here."

" Yes, I'm at leisure. What can I do for you ? Smoke ? "

" No ; I can't to-day. The fact is, I've a bad tooth, and smoking troubles it."

" Indeed ? Let me see it. I'm a bit of a dentist."

" Are you ? That's fortunate, for it aches sadly, and our nearest dentist is five miles away."

" Sit right here by the window, where I can have a good light."

Mr. Belford, a physical coward, could not bear pain ; and though he was unwilling to be under obligations to one whom he considered a mere boy, he sat down in the proffered chair, and opened his mouth dutifully.

" Ah, yes—*dentes sapentia.* It's quite gone. Shall I take it out for you ? "

" Will it be painful ? "

" No. I'll give you nitrous oxide. Without it it might be very painful, for the tooth is much broken down."

Mr. Belford hesitated. Had he better place himself so utterly at the mercy of this young man ?

" It will pass off in a moment, and leave no ill effects behind. You had better take it."

" Well, I will ; but make it very mild, for I am afraid of these new-fangled notions."

7*

"You need have no fear," said Elmer, bringing up his iron box of nitrous oxide, and selecting a pair of forceps from the mass of instruments in one of his trunks.

"It's very odd. It's the merest chance that I happened to have a pair of forceps. Are you ready now? Put this tube in your mouth, and breathe easily and naturally."

The patient leaned back in the chair, and the amateur stood silently watching him.

"It's a fearful risk, but I'm going to try it. I succeeded with Alma, and I fancy I can with this fool. He was a fool to run right into my arms in this fashion. No wonder—his wisdom tooth was rotten. I'll have it out in a moment."

All this to himself. The patient closed his eyes, and fell into a deep sleep.

"Take it strong. It will not hurt you, and I must keep you quiet till the deed is done."

High science was to be brought to bear upon rascality, and he must move cautiously and quickly. The instant the patient was unconscious, Elmer bent over him and turned back his coat, and from the inside pocket he drew forth a folded paper. He had caught a glimpse of it when he looked in the man's mouth, and on the spur of the moment he had conceived and put into practice this bold stroke of applied science. Making the man comfortable, and giving him a little air with the gas, he opened the paper and spread it wide open before a pile of books in the full sunlight. The patient stirred uneasily. With a breathless motion Elmer plied him with more gas, and he sighed softly and slumbered deeper than ever. With a spring he reached the camera, rolled it up before the paper, and set in a new dry plate. It copied the paper with terrible certainty, and then, without . reading it, Elmer folded the paper up again and restored it to his patient's pocket.

The patient revived. He put his hand in his mouth. The tooth was still there.

" Why, you didn't touch it ? "

" No. I was delayed a bit. Take the gas again."

The man submitted, and inhaled more gas. At the instant he slumbered the forceps were deftly plied and the tooth removed. Bathing the man's face with water, the young dentist watched him closely till he revived again.

" Do you feel better ? "

" Better ! Why I'm not hurt ! Is it really out."

" Yes. There it is in the washbowl."

" You did very well, young man. Excellently. I'm sure I'm much obliged."

" You're welcome," replied Mr. Franklin. "It was a trifling affair."

Repeating his thanks, the visitor put on his hat with its two ribbons and retired.

For an hour or more the youthful son of science worked over his new negatives, and then he quietly closed the shutters and lighted his stereopticon. The first picture he threw upon the wall greatly pleased him. With half-parted lips, a placid smile, and closed eyes, the sleeping Alma lived in shadowy beauty before him.

" Queer such a charming girl should belong to such a fool ! "

Not choice language for a son of pure-eyed science, but history is history, and the truth must be told.

" Now for the paper."

He took Alma's stolen picture from the lantern, and inserted in its place a positive copy of the paper he had captured from her lover. Suddenly there flashed upon the wall a document of the most startling and extraordinary character. He read it through several times before he could bring himself to understand the peculiar nature of the important discovery he had made. Long and earnestly he gazed upon the gigantic writing on the wall, and then he slowly opened one of the shutters, and the magic writing faded away in the rosy light of the setting sun.

A moment after the tea-bell rang. This over, young Mr. Franklin said he must go out for his evening constitutional. He wished to be alone. The events of the day, the discoveries he had

made, and, more than all, Alma's grief and silence
at the supper-table, disturbed him. He wished
more air, more freedom to think over these things
and to devise some plan for future action.

Alma. What of her? Was he not growing to
like her—perhaps love her? And she was engaged to that—that—he could not think of him
with patience. The chimney, the two in the
photo, and the strange paper: what did they all
mean? Why were both father and daughter in
such evident distress? He pondered these things
as he walked through the shadowy lanes, and then,
about eight o'clock, he returned, in a measure com-
posed and serene.

There was a light in the parlor, and he went in
and found Alma alone.

" Oh, Elmer! I'm glad you've come. It's very
lonely here. Father has gone to bed quite ill, and
Lawrence asked me to sit up till he returned.
He's gone down to the village on some business.
I can't see why he should. The stores are closed
and the last train has gone."

She made a place for him on the sofa, and he
sat down beside her. For some time they talked
indifferently upon various matters—the weather,
the heat of the day, and like trivialities.

Suddenly she turned upon him, and said, with
ill-suppressed excitement :

" What did you do with it, Elmer ? "

"Do with what?"

"The picture."

"Oh, yes—the lantern slide. I wish I had never made it. It's upstairs in my room."

"You didn't know it was Alice Green?"

".No. How should I? I did not know who either of the people was till the picture was thrown upon the wall."

"Do you know now—know both of them, I mean?"

"Yes—I think I do. One was Mr.——"

"Yes, Elmer, you may as well say it. It was Lawrence."

Elmer could think of nothing to say, and wisely said nothing. After a brief pause Alma said slowly, as if talking to herself:

"It was a cruel thing to do."

"I did not mean to be cruel."

"Oh, my dear—cousin, don't think of it in that way. It was Lawrence who was so cruel."

"Yes. It was not very gentlemanly; but perhaps he does not care for—for this person."

"He does. The picture was only confirmation of what I had heard before. I've done with him," she added in a sort of suppressed desperation. "I'm going to break our engagement this very night. I know it will nearly break my heart, and father will be very angry; but, Elmer, come nearer; let me tell you about it. I'm afraid of him. He has such an evil eye, and you remember the chimney—the day you came—I thought he would kill you, he was so angry."

Evidently she was in sore trouble. Even her language was marked by doubt and difficulty.

"Advise me, Elmer. Tell me what to do. I hardly know which way to turn, and I'm so lonely. Father is busy every day, and I can't talk to him. And Lawrence—I dare not trust him."

Here she began to cry softly, and hid her face in her handkerchief. The son of science was perplexed. What should he do or say? All this was new to him. That a young and pretty girl should appeal to him with such earnestness disconcerted him, and he did not know how to act. A problem in triangulation or knotty question in physics would have charmed him and braced him up for any work. This was so new and so peculiar that he said, "Don't cry, cousin," and repented it at once as a silly speech.

"I must. It does me good."

"Then I would."

Thereupon they both laughed heartily and felt better. He recovered his wits at once.

"Do you think you really love him?"

The man of science is himself again.

"No, I don't."

"Then—well, it's hardly my place to say it."

"Then break the engagement. That's what

you mean.   I intend to do so ; but, Elmer, I wish
you could be here with me."

" It would be impossible.   Oh ! I've an idea."

" Have you ?   There ! I knew you would help
me.   You are so bright, Elmer, and so kind——"

He nipped her enthusiasm in the bud.

" Do you think you could telegraph to me from
your pocket ? "

" I don't know what you mean."

" You know the letters now perfectly, and if you
had your hand on an armature, you could send
off messages quickly ? "

" Yes.   You know I learned the alphabet in one
day, and it's nearly a week since you put up that
line to my room.   Think how we have talked with
it already.   And you remember the tea-table,
when the Lawsons and the Stebbens were here.
Didn't I answer all your questions about Minna
Lawson, while I was talking with her, by tapping
on the table with a spoon ? "

" Yes.   So far so good ; but now I'm going to
try a most dangerous and difficult piece of scientific work, and you must help me.   My plan is for
you to keep in telegraphic communication with me
while the interview goes on.   Then, if he is insulting or troublesome, you can call me."

" How bright of you, Elmer.   If Lawrence had
been half so good and kind and bright—if he knew
half so much—I might have loved him longer."

" Wait a bit, and I'll get the lines."

" May I go too ? "

" Oh, yes ; come."

The two went softly up the hall-stairs, through the long entry to the L, and into Elmer's room. They put the lamp on a table, and Elmer dragged forth from the scientific confusion of the place a collection of telegraphic apparatus of all kinds.

" There's the battery. That I'll keep here. There is the recording instrument. That I'll keep here also. Now you want a small armature to open and close the current. Wait a bit ! I'd better make one."

Alma sat down on a box, and her new Lohen-grin set to work with shears and file to make something that would answer for an armature and still be small enough to hide in the hand. Cutting off two small pieces of insulated copper wire, he bound them together side by side at one end. The loose ends he separated by crowding a bit of rubber between them, and then with the file and his knife he removed a part of the insulating covering till the bright copper showed at the tips of each wire.

" There ! You can hide that in the pocket of your dress, or hold it in your hand even. When you wish to close the circuit, pinch the wires, and they will touch each other. When you withdraw the pressure the rubber will push them apart."

Alma declared she could do it easily, and the armature having been connected with the wires and the battery, they both prepared to go to the parlor.

Down the stairs they crept, slowly unwinding two delicate coils of insulated wire as they went, and pushing them back against the wall well out of sight. When they came to the mats Alma lifted them up, and Elmer laid the wires down, and then the mats covered them from sight.

" Now, you sit here, in a comfortable chair, and hide the wires in the folds of your dress. I'll lead them off over the carpet behind you, and unless the—Lawrence is brighter than I think he is, he'll not find them."

These mysterious operations were hardly completed before the door-bell rang and Lawrence came in. He did not seem particularly pleased to find Mr. Franklin sitting up with Alma, and the meeting was not very cordial. After a few unimportant remarks Mr. Franklin said that he must retire.

" I'd like to know, miss, what that puppy said to you. He's been here all the evening, I dare say."

" He has, Lawrence ; but I will not have my friends spoken of in that way."

" Your friends, indeed ! What do you intend to do about it."

Meanwhile her hand, persistently kept in her pocket, nervously moved the electric armature, and a sudden twinge of pain startled her. Her finger, caught between the wires, felt the shock of a returning current. Suddenly the pain flashed again, and she understood it. Elmer was replying to her. She forced herself to read his words by the pain the current caused her, and she spelled out:

"Keep cool. Don't fear him."

"Seems to me you're precious silent, miss."

"One might well keep silent while you use such language as you do, Lawrence Belford."

"Who's a better right?"

"No man has a right not to be a gentleman, and as for your right, I have decided to withdraw it."

"What do you mean?" he cried, in sudden anger.

She drew her hand out of her pocket, slowly took off her engagement ring, and said,

"That."

"Oh! We'll have none of that. You may put your ring on again."

"I shall never wear it again."

"Yes, you will."

"I shall not."

"Look here, Miss Denny. We'll have no nonsense. You are going to marry me next week. I suppose you know that mortgage is to be foreclosed on Monday, and you and your father will be beggars. I know how to stop all this, and I can do it. Marry me, and go to New York with me on Wednesday, and the mortgage will be withdrawn."

" We may find the will before that."

" Oh ! You may, you may. You and your father have been searching for that will these ten years. You haven't found it yet, and you won't."

Alma, under any ordinary circumstances, would have quailed before this man. As it was, those trails of copper wire down her dress kept her busy. She rapidly sent off through them nearly all that was said, and her knight of the battery sat upstairs copying it off alone in his room, and almost swearing with anger and excitement.

Suddenly, the messages stopped. He listened sharply at the door. Not a sound. The old house was as still as a grave. Several minutes passed, and nothing came. What had happened ? Had he cut the wires ? Had Alma fainted ? Suddenly, the sounder spoke out clear and sharp in the silent room :

" Elmer, come ! "

He seized a revolver from the bureau, and thrusting it into his pocket, tore off the white strip of paper that had rolled out of the instrument, and with it in his hand he went quickly down-stairs. He opened the door without knocking, and advanced into the middle of the room.

The moment he entered, Alma sprang up from her seat, pulling out the two wires as she did so, and throwing her arm about the young man, she cried out in an agony of fear and shame :

" Oh, Elmer, Elmer! Take me away! Take me to my father ! "

He supported her with his right arm, and turned to face her assailant with the crumpled ribbon of paper still in his hand.

" What does this mean, sir ? Have you been ill-treating my cousin ? "

" Go to bed, boy. It's very late for school-children to be up."

" Your language is insulting, sir. I repeat it, What have you said or done to Miss Denny ? "

" Oh ! Come away ! come away, Elmer ! "

" None of your business, you puppy."

" There is no need to ask what you have said, sir. I know every word and have made a copy of it."

" Ah ! Listening, were you ? "

" No, sir. Miss Denny has told me. Do you see those wires ? They will entangle you yet and trip you up."

" Come away, Elmer. Come away."

" For the present I will retire, sir ; but, mark me, your game is nearly up."

" By, by, children. Good-night. Remember your promise, Miss Denny. The carriage will be all ready."

Without heeding this last remark, Elmer, with

his cousin on his arm, withdrew. As they closed the door the telegraph wires caught in the carpet and broke. The man saw them, and picking one up, he examined it closely.

Suddenly he dropped it and turned ashen pale. With all his bravado, he quailed before those slender wires upon the carpet. He did not understand them. He guessed they might be some kind of telegraph, but beyond this everything was vague and mysterious, and they filled him with guilty alarm and terror.

CHAPTER II.—CONCLUSION.

THE events of the last chapter happened on the night of Friday, July —, 1880. The following day, Saturday, broke calm, clear, and warm. Elmer awoke early, carefully looked out of a crack in his window curtain, and found that the chimney-builder's room was empty.

"The enemy has flown. I wonder if Alma is up?"

He uncovered a small telegraphic armature and sounder standing on the window-seat, and touched it gently. In an instant there was a response, and Alma replied that she was up and dressed and would soon be down.

She met him in the library, smiling, and apparently happy.

"Oh, Elmer, he has gone away. He left a note on the breakfast-table, saying that he had gone to New York, and that he should not return till Monday or Tuesday."

"That's very good ; but I think it means mischief."

Just here the breakfast-bell rang. The table was set for four, but Alma and Elmer were the only ones who could answer the call, and they sat down to the table alone. They talked of various matters of little consequence, and when the meal was over Elmer announced that as the day was quiet, he should make a little photographing expedition about the neighborhood.

"My visit here is now more than a quarter over, and I wish to take home some photos of the place. Will you not go with me ? "

"With all my heart, if I can leave father. But please not talk of going home yet. I hope you will not go till things are settled. We want you, Elmer. You are so wise and strong, and—you know what I mean."

"Perhaps I do. At any rate I'm not going till I have paid up that Belford for his insults."

"Oh, let's not talk of him to-day."

This was eminently wise. They had better enjoy the day of peace that was before them. The

shadow of the coming events already darkened
their lives, though they knew it not.   Mr. Denny
was so much better that he could spare Alma, and
about ten o'clock she appeared, paper umbrella in
hand, at the porch, and Elmer soon joined her bearing a small camera, a case of the wonderful emul-
sion bromide plates, and a light wooden tripod.

The two spent the morning happily in each
other's company, and at one o'clock returned to
dinner with quite a number of negatives of various
objects of interest about the place.   After dinner
the young man retreated to his room to prepare
for the battle that he felt sure would rage on the
following Monday.

He did not know all the circumstances of the
trouble that had invaded the family, but he felt
sure that the confidential clerk intended some terrible shame or exposure that in some way concerned
his cousin Alma.   So it was he came to call himself her Lohengrin, come to fight her battles, not
with a sword, but with the telegraph, the camera,
and the micro-lantern.

The Sabbath passed quietly, and the Monday
came.   After breakfast the student retreated to
his room and tried to study, but could not.

About ten o'clock he heard a carriage of some
kind stop before the house.   His room being at
the rear, he could not see who had come, and
thinking that it might be merely some stray visi-

tor, and that at least it did not concern him, he turned to his books and made another attempt to read.

After some slight delay he heard the carriage drive away, and the old house became very still. Then he heard a door open down-stairs, and a moment after one of the maids knocked at his door.

" Would Mr. Franklin kindly come down-stairs? Mr. Denny wished to see him in the library."

He would come at once ; and picking up a number of unmounted photographs from the table, he prepared to go down-stairs. He hardly knew why he should take the pictures just then. There seemed no special reason why he should show them to Mr. Denny ; still, an indefinite feeling urged him to take them with him.

The library was a small room, dark, with heavy book-shelves against the walls, and crowded with tables, desk, and easy-chairs. There was a student-lamp on the centre-table, and in a corner stood a large iron safe. Mr. Denny was seated at the table with his back to the door, and with his head supported by his hand and arm. He did not seem to notice the arrival of his visitor, and Elmer advanced to the table and laid the photographs upon it.

" I am glad you have come, Mr. Franklin. I wish to talk with you. I wish to tell you something. A great affliction has fallen upon us, and I wish you, as our guest, to be prepared for it. I

8

think I can trust you, Elmer Franklin. I remember your mother, my boy. You have her features —and I will trust you for her sake. We are ruined."

" How, sir ? How is that possible, with all your property ? "

" Not one cent of my property—not a foot of ground, or a single brick, or piece of shafting in the mills—belongs to me."

" This is terrible, sir. How did it happen ? "

" It is a short and sad story. I was my father's only child, and there were no other heirs. My father's last illness was very sudden, and he left no will. He told me when he died that he had left everything to me. We never found any will that would bear out this assertion. However, the ordinary process of law gave me the property, and I thought myself secure. Suddenly a will was found, in which all the property was left to a distant relative in New York, and I was merely mentioned with some trifling gift. I contested the will and lost the case. It was an undoubted will, and in my father's own handwriting, and dated more than a year before he died and when I was rusticating from college. I thought I must needs sow my wild oats, and day after to-morrow I pay for them all by total beggary. The devisee, by the will, acted very strangely about the property. He did not disturb me for a very long time. He probably feared to do so ; and then he made a mortgage of one hundred thousand dollars on the property, took the money, and went abroad."

" And he left you here in possession ? "

" Yes. The interest on the mortgage became due. There was no one to pay for it, and they even had the effrontery to come to me. I refused again and again, and every time the interest was added to the mortgage till it rolled up to an enormous amount. Meanwhile the devisee died, penniless, in Europe, and on Wednesday Abrams, the lawyer who holds the mortgage, is to take possession of everything—and we—we are to go—I know not whither."

For a few moments there was a profound silence. in the room. The elder man mourned his dreadful fate, and the son of science was ready to shout for joy. Restraining himself with an effort, he said, not without a tremor in his voice :

" And have you searched for any other will ? "

" That is an idle question, my son. We have searched these years. Then, too, just as I need a staff for my declining years, it breaks under me."

" You refer to Mr. Belford, sir ? "

" Yes. Since I injured my foot in the mill, I have trusted all my affairs to him, and now I sometimes think he is playing me false. Even now, when all this trouble has come upon me, he is absent, and I have no one to consult, nor do I find any to aid or comfort me."

" Perhaps I can aid you, sir."

" I do not know. I fear no one can avail us now."

" May I be very frank with you, sir ? "

" Certainly. I am past all pride or fear. There can be nothing worse now."

" I think, sir, you have placed too much confidence in that man. He is not trustworthy."

" How do you know ? Can you prove it ? "

" Yes, sir. You remember the new chimney ? "

" Yes ; but he explained that, and collected all the money that had been paid on the supposed extra height of the chimney."

" That was very easy, sir, for he had it in his own pocket. I met some of the work-people in the village, and casually asked them how high the chimney was to be, and every man gave the real height. Mr. Belford lied to you about it, and pocketed the difference, between his measurements and mine. Of course, when detected he promptly restored the money, and thought himself lucky to have escaped so easily. More than that, he claimed that the chimney was capped with stone. It is not. It is brick to the top, and the upper courses were rubbed over with colored plaster."

" I can hardly believe it. Besides, how can you ' prove it ? "

" That will, sir. Look at it carefully."

So saying, Elmer selected a photograph from those on the table and presented it to Mr. Denny.

The old gentleman looked at it carefully for a few moments, and then said with an air of conviction—

" It is a perfect fraud. I had no idea that the man was such a thief."

" Yes, sir. Look at that bare place where the plaster has fallen off. You can see the bricks."

" Oh, I can see. There is no need to explain the picture. Have you any more ? "

" Yes, sir ; quite a number. I'm glad I brought them with me."

Mr. Denny turned them over slowly, and commented briefly upon them.

" That's the house. Very well done, my boy. That's the mill. Excellent. I should know it at once. And—eh ! what's that ? The batting-mill ? "

" Yes, sir. That's the new building going up beyond the mill-pond."

" Great heavens ! What an outrageous fraud ! Mr. Belford told me it was nearly done. He has drawn almost all the money for it already, and according to this picture only one story is up. When was this picture taken ? "

" On Saturday, sir. Alma was with me. She will tell you."

Mr. Denny rang a small bell that stood at his elbow, and a maid came to the door.

"Will you call Miss Denny, Anna?"

The maid retired, and in a moment or two Alma appeared. She seemed pale and dejected, and she sat down at once as if weary.

"What is it, father? Any new troubles?"

"Were you with your cousin when he took this photograph?"

She looked at it a moment, and then said wearily:

"Yes. It's the batting-mill."

Just here the door opened, and Mr. Belford, hat and travelling bag in hand, as if just from the station, entered the room. The two men looked up in undisguised amazement, but Alma cast her eyes upon the floor, and her face seemed to put on a more ashen hue than ever.

"Ah! excuse me. I did not mean to intrude. I'm just from New York, and I have been so successful that I hastened to lay the news before you."

"What have you to say, Mr. Belford," said Mr. Denny coldly. "There are none but friends here, and you need not fear to speak."

Mr. Franklin hastily gathered up the pictures together, and rolling them up, put them in his pocket, with the mental remark that he "knew of one who was not a friend—no, not much."

"I have arranged everything," said Mr. Belford,

with sublime audacity. "The note has been taken up. I have even obtained a release of the mortgage, and here is the cancelled note and the release. To-morrow I will have it recorded."

"We are in no mood for pleasantry, Mr. Belford. The sheriff was here to-day, and Abrams is to take possession on Wednesday."

"Oh, I knew that. He did not get my telegram in time, or he would have saved you all this unnecessary annoyance. And now everything is quite clear, and there is Abrams's release in full."

He took out a carefully folded paper, and gave it to Mr. Denny. He read it in silence, and then said :

"It seems to be quite correct. We——"

Alma suddenly dropped her head upon her breast, and slid to the floor in a confused heap. She thought she read in that fatal receipt her death-warrant. Nature rebelled, and mercifully took away her senses.

Elmer sprang to her rescue, but Mr. Belford intruded himself.

"It is my place, Mr. Franklin. She is to be my wife."

The dreary day crept to its end. Alma recovered, and retired to her room. Mr. Denny, overcome by the excitement of the interview, was quite ill, and the visitor, oppressed with a sense of partial

defeat, took a long walk through the country.
The enemy had made such an extraordinary movement that for the time he was disconcerted, and he
wished to be alone, that he might think over the
situation.   About six o'clock in the afternoon he
returned looking bright and calm, as if he thought
out his problem and had nerved himself up to do
and dare all in behalf of the woman he loved.   He
went quietly to his room and began his preparations
for a vigorous assault upon the enemy.

He rolled out his magic-lantern into the middle
of the room, drew up the curtains at the window
that faced Mr. Belford's chamber, and prepared to
adjust the apparatus to a new and most singular style of lantern projections.   He had hardly
finished the work to his satisfaction before he
heard Alma's knock at the door.   He hastily drew
down the curtains, and then invited her to come
in.

She opened the door and appeared upon the
threshold, the picture of resigned and heavy sorrow.   She had evidently been weeping, and the
dark dress in which she had arrayed herself seemed
to intensify the look of anguish on her face.   The
son of science was disconcerted.   He did not know
what to say, and, with great wisdom, he said nothing.

She entered the room without a word, and sat
wearily down on a trunk.   Elmer quickly rolled

out the great easy-chair so that it would face the
open western window.

"Sit here, Miss Denny. This is far more comfortable."

"Oh, Elmer! Have you too turned against
me?"

"Not knowingly. Sit here where there is more
air, and before this view and this beautiful sunset."

She rose, and with a forlorn smile took the great
chair, and then gazed absently out of the window
upon the charming landscape, brilliant with the
glow of the setting sun. Elmer meanwhile went
on with his work, and for a little space neither
spoke. Then she said, with a faint trace of impatience in her voice—

"What are you doing, Elmer?"

"Preparing for war."

"It is useless. It is too late."

"Think so?"

"Yes. Everything has been settled, and in a
very satisfactory manner—at least father is satis-
fied, and I suppose I ought to be."

She smiled and held out her hand to him.

"How can I ever thank you, cousin Elmer?
You will not forget me when I am gone."

"Forget you, Alma! That was unkind."

He took her hand, glanced at the diamond ring
upon her finger, and looking down upon her as she

8*

lay half reclining in the great chair, he said, with an effort, as if the words pained him :

" Alma, you have surrendered to him."

She looked up with a startled expression, and said :

" What do you mean ? "

" You have renewed your engagement with Mr. Belford ? "

" Yes—of course I have.   He—he is to be my husband."

" On Wednesday."

" Yes.   How did you know ? "

Instead of replying he turned to a drawer and drew forth a long ribbon of white paper.   Holding it to the light, near the window, he began to read the words printed in dots and lines upon it.

" Here is your own confession.   Here are all the messages you sent me from the parlor, when you broke your engagement with him."

" Oh, Elmer ! Did you save that ? Destroy it— destroy it at once.   If he should find it, he would never forgive me."

"You need not fear.   I shall not destroy it, and it shall never cause you any trouble."

She had risen in her excitement, and stood upon her feet.   Suddenly she flushed a rosy red, and a strange light shone in her eyes.   The sun had sunk behind the hills, and it had grown dark.   As the shadows gathered in the room a strange, mystic light fell on the wall before her. A picture—dim, ghostly, gigantic, and surpassingly beautiful,— met her astonished eyes. She gazed at it with a beating heart, awed into silence by its mystery and its unearthly aspect. What was it? What did it mean? By what magic art had he conjured up this vision? She stood with parted lips gazing at it, while her bosom rose and fell with her rapid, excited breathing. Suddenly she threw her arms above her head, and with a cry fell back upon the chair.

" Oh, Elmer! My heart——"

He had been gazing absently out of the window at the fading twilight, and hearing her cry of pain, he turned hastily and said :

" Alma, what is it? Are you ill?"

He caught sight of the picture on the wall. He understood it at once, and went to the stereopticon that stood at the other end of the room and opened it. The lamp was burning brightly, and he put it out and closed the door. Then he drew out the glass slide, held it a moment to the light to make sure that it was Alma's portrait, and then he kissed it passionately, and shivered it into fragments upon the hearthstone.

She heard the breaking glass, and rose hastily and turned toward him.

" Elmer, that was cruel. Why did you destroy it?"

" Because it told too much."

" It was my picture ? "

" Yes. I confess with shame that I stole it when you were asleep under the influence of the gas I gave you. It happened to be in the lantern when you came in."

" And so I saw it pictured on the wall ? "

" Yes. In that way did it betray me. Forget it, Alma. Forget me. Forget everything. Forget that I ever came here."

" That I cannot."

" You will be married soon and go away. I presume we may never meet again."

" Oh, Elmer, forgive me. I am the one to be forgiven. I am alone to blame for all this sorrow. I thought I alone should suffer. But—but, Elmer, you will not forget me, and you see—you must see that what I do is for the best. It is the only way. I cannot see my father beggared."

The clear-headed son of science seemed to be losing his self-control. This was all so new, so exciting, so different from the calm and steady flow of his student-life, that he knew not what to say or do. He began to turn over his books and papers in a nervous manner, as if trying to win back control of his own tumultuous thoughts. Fortunately Alma came to his rescue.

" Elmer, hear me."

" Yes," he said with an effort. " Tell me about

it; then perhaps we can understand each other better."

" I will. Come and sit by me. It grows dark, and I—well, it is no matter. It will do me good to speak of it."

" Yes, do. Sorrow shared is divided by half."

" And joy shared is doubled," she added. " But we will not talk of ' the might have been.' "

Then she paused and looked out on the gathering night for some minutes in silence. Elmer sat at her feet upon a low stool, and waited till she should speak.

" Elmer, say that you will forgive me, whatever happens. No matter how dark it looks for me, forgive me—and—do not forget me. I couldn't bear that. On Wednesday I am to be married to Mr. Belford. It is the only way by which I can save my father. There seems no help for it, and I consented this afternoon. Mr. Belford took up the mortgage, and I am to be his reward."

Elmer heard her through in silence, and then he stood up before her, and his passion broke out in fury upon her.

"Alma Denny, you are a fool."

She cowered before him, and covered her face with her hands.

" Have you no sense? Can you not see the wide pit of deceit that is spread before you? Do you believe what he says? Will you walk into perdition to save your father?"

"Oh, Elmer! Elmer! Spare me, spare me, for my father's sake!"

Her sobs and tears choked her utterance, and she sank away into the depths of the chair, in shame and terror, thankful that the darkness hid her from his view. Still his righteous indignation blazed upon her hotly.

"Where have you lived? What have you done, that you should be so deceived by this man? How can you save your father? If you cannot find that missing will, of what avail is this withdrawal of the mortgage?"

"I do not know. Oh, Elmer! I am weak, and I have no mother, and my father! I must save him if I can—at any price."

"You cannot save him. The devisee who held the will has heirs. They can still claim the property. Besides, how could Mr. Belford pay off that mortgage? Depend upon it there is nothing but fraud there."

She fainted suddenly away, and slid down upon the floor at his feet. He called two of the maids, and with their help he took her to her room and placed her upon her own bed. Then, bidding them care for her properly, he returned to his own room, and the heavy night fell down on the sorrowful house.

Far away in the northwest climbed up a ragged mass of sombre clouds. Afar off the deep voice of the thunder muttered fitfully. The son of science drew up his curtains and looked out on the coming storm. There was a solemn hush and calm in the air. Nature seemed resting, and nerving herself for the warfare of the elements.

He too had need of calm. He drew a chair to the window, and sitting astride of it, he rested his arms upon the back, and his chin upon his folded hands, and for an hour watched the lightning flash from ragged cloud to ragged cloud, and gave himself to deep and anxious thought. The thunder grew nearer and louder. The dark veil of clouds blotted out the stars one by one. The roar of the water falling over the dam at the mill seemed to fill all the air with its murmur. Every leaf and flower hung motionless.

He heard the village clock strike nine, with loud, deep notes that seemed almost at hand. Every nerve of his body seemed strung to electric tension, and all nature tuned to a higher pitch as if dark and terrible things were abroad in the night.

He heard a sound of closing blinds and windows. The servants were shutting up the house, and preparing it for the storm.

One of them knocked at his door, and asked if she should come in and close his windows.

He opened the door, thanked her, and said he

would attend to it himself. As he closed the door and stepped back into the room, he stood upon something and there was a little crash. Thinking it might be glass, he lit a candle and looked for the broken object, whatever it might be.

It was Alma's engagement ring, broken in twain. It had slipped from her nerveless finger when they took her to her room. With a gesture of impatience, he picked up the fragments, and threw them, diamond and all, out of the window into the garden below.

Then for another hour he sat alone in the darkness of his room, watchful and patient. He drew up the curtain toward Alma's room. There was a light there, and he sat gazing at her white curtain till the light was extinguished. The other lights were all put out one after the other, and then it became very still.

The clock struck ten. The gathering storm climbed higher up the western sky. The lightning flashed brighter and brighter. There was a sigh in the tree tops as if the air stirred uneasily.

Suddenly there was another light. Mr. Belford's curtain was brightly illuminated by his candle. Elmer moved his chair so that he could watch the window, and waited patiently till the light was put out. Then he saw the curtain raised and the window drawn down.

"All right, my boy! That's just what I wanted.

Nemesis has a clear road, and her shadowy sword shall reach you. Now for the closed circuit alarm.''

He silently pulled off his shoes, and then, with the tread of a cat, he felt about his room till he found on the table two delicate coils of fine insulated wire, and a couple of tacks. Carefully opening the door, he crept down stairs and through the hall to the door of the library. The door was closed, and kneeling down on the mat he pushed a tack into the door near the jamb and stuck the other in the door-post. From one to another he stretched a bit of insulated wire. Then, aided by the glare of the flashes of lightning, that had now grown bright and frequent, he laid the wires under the mat and along the floor to the foot of the stairs. Then in his stockinged feet he crept upward, dropping the wires over into the well of the stairway as he went. In a moment or two the wires were traced along the floor of the upper entry and under the door into his room. Here they were secured to a small battery, and connected with a tiny electric bell that stood on the mantle shelf. To stifle its sound in case it rang, he threw his straw hat over the bell, and then he felt sure that at least one part of his work was done.

Louder and louder rolled the thunder. The lightning flashed brightly and lit up the bare, mean little room where the wretch cowered and shivered in the bed, sleepless and fearful he knew not why.

He feared the storm and the night. He feared everything. His guilty heart made terrors out of the night and nature's healthful workings. The very storm, blessed harbinger of clearer days and sweeter airs, terrified him.

There was a sound of rushing wind in the air. A more vivid flash blinded him. He sat up in bed and stopped his coward ears to drown the splendid roll of the thunder. Another flash seemed to fill the room.

Ah! What was that? His eyes seemed to start from their sockets in horror.

There, written in gigantic letters of fire upon the wall, glowed and burned a single word:

FRAUD!

He stared at it and rubbed his eyes. It would not be winked out. There was a loud crash of thunder and a furious dash of rain against the window; then another blinding stroke of lightning. He drew the clothing over his head in abject terror. Again the thunder rolled as if in savage comment on the writing on the wall:

It was a mistake, a delusion. He would face the horrid accusation.

It was gone, and in its place was a picture. It seemed the top of——

Ah! It was that chimney. Already the false

stucco had fallen off, and there, pictured upon his wall, in lines of fire, were the evidences of his fraud and crime.

He sprang from the bed with an oath and looked out of the window. Darkness everywhere. The beating rain on the window pane ran down in blinding rivulets. A vivid flash of lightning illuminated the garden and the house. Not a living thing was stirring. He turned toward the bed. The terrible picture had gone. With a muttered curse upon his weak, disordered nerves, he crept into bed and tried to sleep.

Suddenly the terrible writing glowed upon the wall again, and he fairly screamed with fright and horror :

MURDER !

He writhed and turned upon the bed in mortal agony. He stared at the letters of the awful word with ashen lips and chattering teeth. What hideous dream was this ? Had his reason reeled ? Could it play him phantom tricks like this ? Or was it an avenging angel from heaven writing his crimes upon the black night ?

" Great God ! What was that ? "

The writing disappeared, and in its place stood a picture of his wretched victim and himself. Her fair, innocent face looked down upon him from the darkness, and he saw his own form beside her.

He raved with real madness now. Great drops of perspiration gathered on his face. He dared not face those beautiful eyes so calmly gazing at him. Where had high Heaven gained such knowledge of him? How could it punish him with such awful cruelty?

" Hell and damnation have come," he screamed in frantic terror. The thunder rolled in deep majesty, and none heard him. The wind and rain beat upon the house, and his ravings disturbed no one.

" Take it away! Take it away!" he cried in sheer madness and agony.

It would not move. The lightning only made the picture more startling and awful. The sweet and beautiful face of Alice Green lived before him in frightful distinctness, and his very soul seemed to burn to cinder before her serene, unearthly presence.

It was her ghost revisiting the earth. Was it to always thus torment him?

" Thank God! It has gone."

The room became pitch dark, and he fell back upon the pillow in what seemed to him a bloody sweat. He could not sleep, and for some time he lay trembling on the bed and trying to collect his senses and decide whether he was in possession of his reason or not.

Suddenly there was a flash of light, and a new vision sprang into existence before him.

An angel in long white robes seemed to be flying through the air toward him, and above her head she held a sword. Beneath her feet was the word " NEMESIS ! " in letters of glowing fire.

The poor wretch rose up in bed, kneeled down upon the mattress, and facing the gigantic figure that seemed to float in the air above him, cried aloud in broken gasps :

" Pardon !   For—Christ's sake."

He threw up his arms and screamed in delirious terror.

The angel advanced through the air toward him and grew larger and taller.   She seemed ready to strike him to the ground—and she was gone.

He fell forward flat on his face, and tears gushed from his eyes in torrents.   For a while he lay thus moaning and crying, and then he rose, staggered to the wash basin, bathed his face with cold water, and crept shivering and trembling into bed.

The storm moved slowly away.   The lightning grew less frequent, and the thunder rolled in more subdued tones.   The wind subsided, but the rain fell steadily and drearily.   One who watched heard the clock strike twelve and then one.

Slowly the laggard hours slipped away in silence. The rain fell in monotonous showers.   The darkness hung like a pall over everything.

The wretch in his bed tossed in sleepless misery.

He hardly dared look at the blackness of the night, for fear some new vision might affright him with ghostly warnings. What had he better do? Another night in this haunted room would drive him insane. Had he not better fly—leave all and escape out of sight in the hiding darkness? Better abandon the greater prize, take everything in reach, and fly from scenes so terrible.

He rose softly, dressed completely, took a few essentials from his table, did them up in a bundle, and then like a cat he crept out of the room, never to return. The house was pitch dark and as silent as a tomb. He had no need of a light, and, feeling his way along with his hands on the wall, he stole down stairs and through the hall till he reached the library door. With cautious fingers he turned the handle in silence and pushed the door open. It seemed to catch on the threshold, but it was only for an instant, and then he boldly entered the room.

Placing his bundle upon the table, he took out a small bunch of keys, and with his hands outstretched before him he felt for the safe. It was easily found, and then he put in the key, unlocked the door, and swung it open. With familiar fingers he pulled out what he knew were mere bills and documents, and then he found the small tin box in which—

A blinding glare, an awful flash of overpowering light blazed before him. His eyes seemed put out by its bewildering intensity, and a little scream of terror escaped from his lips. A hand seized him by the collar and dragged him over backward upon the floor. The blazing, burning light filled all the room with a glare more terrible than the lightning. He recovered his sight, and saw Nemesis standing above him, revolver in hand, and with a torch of magnesium wire blazing in horrid flames above his head.

" Stir hand or foot, and—you understand. There are six chambers, and I'm a good shot."

"Let me up, you fool, or I'll kill you."

"Oh! You surprise me, Mr. Belford. I thought it was a common robber."

" No, it is not—so lower your pistol."

" No, sir. You may rise, but make the slightest resistance, and I'll blow your brains into fragments. Sit in that chair, and when I've secured you properly, I'll hear any explanation you may make. Your conduct is very singular, Mr. Belford, to say the least. That's it. Sit down in the armchair. Now I'm going to tie you into it, and on the slightest sign of resistance I shall fire."

The poor, cowed creature sank into the chair, and the son of science placed his strange lamp upon the table. With the revolver still in hand, he procured a match and lit a candle on the table. Then he extinguished his torch and the overpowering light gave place to a more agreeable gloom. Then he

took from his pocket a tiny electric bell and a little
battery made of a small ink bottle.   Then he drew
forth a small roll of wire, and securing one end to
the battery, with the revolver still in hand, he
walked round the chair three times and bound the
thief into it with the slender wire.

"Stop this fooling, boy! Lower your revolver, and let me explain matters."

"No, sir.   When I have you fast so that you
can do no harm, I talk with you—not before.
Hold back your head.   That's it.   Rest it against
the chair while I draw this wire over your throat."

"For God's sake, stop! Do you intend to gar-
rote me?"

"No.   I only mean to make you secure."

"This won't hold me long.   I'll break your
wires in a flash, you little fool."

"No, you will not.   The moment the wire is
parted that bell will ring, and I shall begin firing,
and keep it up till you are disabled or dead."

The man swore savagely, but the cold thread of
insulated wire over his throat thrilled his every
nerve.   It seemed some magic bond, mysterious,
wonderful, and dreadful.   This cool man of science
was an angel of awful and incomprehensible power.
His lamp of such mystic brilliance and that battery quite unnerved his coward heart.   What awful torture, what burning flash of lightning might
not rend him to blackened fragments if the wires

were broken! To such depths of puerile igno-
rance and terror did the wretch sink in his guilty
fancy. He dared not move a muscle lest the wire
break. The very thought of it filled him with un-
speakable agony. The son of science placed himself before his prisoner. With the revolver at easy
rest, he said :

"Mr. Belford, I am going to call help. Do not
move while I open the door."

In mortal terror the wretch turned his head
round to see what was going on. He managed to
get a glimpse of the room without breaking the
wire round his throat, and he saw the young man
stoop to the floor at the door and pick up something. Then he made some strange and rapid motions with the fingers of his right hand, while the
left still steadied the revolver.

For several minutes nothing happened. The
two men glared at each other in silence, and then
there was a sound of opening doors. One closed
with an echoing slam that resounded strangely
through the old house, and then there were light
footsteps in the hall.

"Oh! Elmer! What is it? What has happened?"

"Nothing very serious—merely a common bur-
glar. I called you because I wished help."

"Yes, I heard the bell, and I read your message

9

in my room by the sound. I dressed as quickly as possible. Is there no danger?"

"No. Stand back. Do not come into the room. Call the men, and let them wake the gardener and his son. You yourself call your father, and bid him dress and come down at once. And, Alma, keep cool and do not be alarmed. I need you, Alma, and you must help me."

Then the house was very still, and the watcher paced up and down before his prisoner in silence. There came a hasty opening of doors, and excited steps and flaring lamps in the hall.

"'Tis the young doctor. Oh! By mighty! Here's troubles!"

"Quiet, men! Keep quiet. Come in. He cannot hurt you."

The three men, shivering and anxious, peered into the room with blanched faces and chattering teeth.

"Have you a rope?"

The calm voice of the speaker reassured them, and all three volunteered to go for one.

"No. One is enough. And one of you had better go to Mr. Denny's room and help him down stairs. You, John, may stop with me."

"Odds! Sir, he will spring at me!"

"Never you fear. He's fastened into the chair. Besides—— "

" Ay, sir, you've the little pet ! That's the kind o' argiment."

" It is a rather nice weapon—six-shooter—Colt's."

Presently, with much clatter, the gardener's son brought a rope, and then, under Mr. Franklin's directions, they bound the man in the chair hand and foot.

A moment after they heard Mr. Denny's crutch stalking down the stairs, and Alma's voice assuring him that there was indeed no danger—no danger at all.

" What does this mean, Mr. Franklin ? " said the old gentleman as he came to the door.

" Burglary, sir. That is all. You need fear nothing. We have secured the man."

Mr. Denny entered the room leaning on Alma's arm. He saw the open safe and the papers strewed upon the floor, and he lifted his hand and shook his head in alarm and trouble.

" A robbery ! Would they ruin me utterly ? Where is the villain ? "

" There, sir."

Alma turned toward the man in the chair, and clung to her father in terror. The old man lifted his crutch as if to strike.

" My curse be upon you and yours."

" Oh, father, come away. Leave the poor wretch. Perhaps he has taken nothing."

The men gathered round in a circle, and Elmer drew near to Alma. She felt his presence near her, and involuntarily put out her hand to touch him.

" My curse fall on you ! Who are you ? What have I done to you—you—viper ? "

The man secured in the chair, and with the wire drawn tightly over his throat, replied not a word.

Elmer advanced toward him, and Alma, with a little cry, tried to hinder him.

" Do not fear. He cannot move. I will release his head, and perhaps you will recognize him."

The wire about his throat was loosened, and the wretch lifted his head into a more comfortable position.

" Ah ! "

" Great Heavens ! It is Mr. Belford ! "

" Yes, sir," said he. " I forgot to put away some papers, and I came down to secure them, and while I was here that wretch surprised me, threatened to murder me, and finally overpowered me and bound me here as you see. If you will ask him to release me, I will get up and explain everything."

" It's a lie," screamed Mr. Denny, lifting his crutch. " I don't believe you—you thief—you róbber ! It's a lie ! "

" Oh, father ! " cried Alma. " Release him— let him go. He. will go away then, and leave us.

He has done wrong ; but let him go.   It must be some awful mistake—some——"

"No!   Never! never! ne—v——"

The word died away on his lips, for on the instant there was a loud ring at the hall door. They all listened in silence.   Again the importunate bell pealed through the echoing house.

"It is some one in distress," said Elmer. "John, do you take a light and go to the door. Ask what is wanted before you loose the chain, and tell them to go away unless it is a case of life or death."

They listened in breathless interest to the confused sounds in the hall.   There was a moving of locks, and then rough voices talking in suppressed whispers.   The candles flared in the cold draught of wind that swept into the room, and the sound of the rain in the trees filled the air.   Then the door closed, and John returned, and in an excited whisper said :

"It's Mr. Jones, the sheriff."

At this word Mr. Belford struggled with his bonds, and in a broken voice he cried :

"Oh, Mr. Denny, spare me ! Let me not be arrested.   I will restore every penny."

"Silence, sir !" said Elmer.   "Not a word till you are spoken to. What does he want, John ?"

"He says he must see Mr. Denny. It's very important—and, oh, sir, he's a'most beside himself, and I wouldn't let him in."   .

"Call him in at once," said Mr. Denny. "It is a most fortunate arrival. The very man we want."

John returned to the hall, and in a moment an old man, gray-haired and wrinkled, but still vigorous and strong, stood before them. He seemed a giant in his huge great-coat, and when he removed his hat his massive head and thick neck seemed almost lionlike.

"Ah! Mr. Sheriff, you have arrived at a most opportune moment. We were just awakened from our beds by this robber. We captured him, and we have him here."

"Beg pardon, sir. Sorry to hear it, but 'twere another errant that brought me here. The widow Green's daughter, Alice, she that was missing, has been found in the mill-race—dead."

They all gave expression to undisguised astonishment, and the prisoner in the chair groaned heavily.

"And I have come for the key of the boat-house, sir, that we may go for the—body, sir."

"How horrible! When did all this happen?"

"We dunno, sir. I'd like the key ter once."

"Certainly—certainly, Mr. Sheriff. But this man—cannot you secure him for the night?"

"Oh, ay. But the child, sir. The boys wants your boat to go for her."

"Poor, poor Alice!" cried Alma, wringing her hands.

"John," said Elmer, "get the key for Mr. Jones. Jake, you and your father can go with the men, and, Mr. Jones, perhaps you had better wait with us, for we have a little matter of importance to settle, and we need you."

"Now," said Mr. Franklin, "I have one or two questions I wish to ask the man, and then, Mr. Jones, you will do us a favor if you will take him away."

"Lawrence Belford, as you value your soul, where did you obtain that will?"

If a bolt from the storm overhead had entered the room, it could not have produced a more startling impression than did this simple question. Mr. Denny dropped his crutch, and raised both hands in astonishment. Alma gave a half suppressed scream, and even the sheriff and John were amazed beyond expression.

The man in the chair made no reply, and presently the breathless silence was broken by the calm voice of the young man repeating his question.

"I found it in the leaves of a book in the old bookcase in the mill office."

"What?" cried Mr. Denny, leaning forward and steadying himself by the table. "My father's will! Did you find it? Release him, John. How can we ever thank you, Mr. Belford? It is the missing will——"

"Oh, Lawrence!" said Alma. "Why did you

not tell us ? why did you not show it ? How much trouble it would have saved."

" Have patience, Alma. Let Mr. Belford rise and bring the will."

" No," said Mr. Franklin. " Hear the rest of the story. Mr. Belford, you destroyed or suppressed that will, did you not ? "

" Yes, I did—damn you ! "

" Good Lord ! " cried the sheriff. " Did ye hear that ?—destroyed it ! That's State's prison."

" Oh, Mr. Franklin, Mr. Denny ! have mercy on me ! Do not let them arrest me."

The poor creature seemed to be utterly cowed and crushed in an instant.

" Marcy ! " said the sheriff, taking out a pair of handcuffs. " It's little marcy ye'll git."

" You ask for mercy ! " cried Mr. Denny, his face livid with passion. " You—you wretch ! Have you not ruined me ? Have you not made my child a beggar, and carried my gray hairs in sorrow to the grave ? You knew the value of this will—and you destroyed it ! Your other crimes are as nothing to this. I could forgive your monstrous frauds in my mills."

Mr. Belford winced and looked surprised.

" Ay ! wince you may. I have found out everything, thanks to—but I'll not couple his name with yours. And the release of the mortgage—have you that ? "

"No, sir. It is in that bag on the table."

The old gentleman eagerly took up the bundle that lay on the table, and began with trembling fingers to open it.

"Wait a moment, Mr. Denny," said Mr. Franklin. "I should like to ask this man a question or two more."

Mr. Denny paused, and there was a profound silence in the room.

"Lawrence Belford, if you are wise, you will speak the truth. That release is a forgery—or at least it has no legal value."

"It is not worth a straw," replied the prisoner with cool impudence; "and on the whole, I'm glad of it. The mortgage will be foreclosed to-morrow."

"Your share will be small, Mr. Belford. I am afraid your partner will find some difficulty in making a settlement with you, unless he joins you in prison."

Mr. Denny sat heavily down in an arm-chair and groaned aloud. In vain Alma, with choking voice, tried to comfort him. The blow was too terrible for words, and for a moment or two there was a painful silence in the room.

Mr. Franklin seemed nervous and excited. He fumbled in his pockets as if in search of something. Presently he advanced toward the old gentleman and said quietly:

9*

" Mr. Denny, can you bear one more piece of news—one more link in this terrible chain of crime ? "

" Yes," he replied slowly.   " There can be noth-ing worse than this.   Speak, my son—let us hear everything."

" I think, sir," said the young man reverently, " that I ought to thank God that He has enabled me to bring such knowledge as He has given me to your service."

Then after a brief pause he added :

" There is the will, sir."   ·

With these words he held out a small bit of sheet glass about two inches square.

" Where ? "   cried Mr. Denny in amazement. " I see nothing."

" There it is—on that piece of glass.   That dusky spot in the centre is a micro-photographic copy of your father's will."

" My son, my son, do not trifle with us in this our hour of trial."

" Far be it from me to do such a thing.   Alma, will you please go to my room and bring down my lantern ?   And John, you may go and help Miss Denny.   Bring a sheet from the spare bed also."

" I do not know what you mean, my son.   You tell me the will is destroyed, and you say you have a copy.   Is it a legal copy ? and how do you know it is really my father's will? Have you read it?"

"Yes, sir. You shall read it too presently. I have already shown it to a lawyer, and he pronounced it correct and perfectly legal."

"But why did you not tell us of it before?"

"I have only had it a few days, sir, and I wished first to crush or capture this robber."

"Hadn't ye better let me take him off, sir?" said the sheriff. "He's done enough to take him afore the grand jury. Besides, we have another little bill against him down in the village."

"No," said Mr. Franklin. "Let him stay and see the will. It may interest him to know that all his villanous plans are utterly overthrown."

"Shut up, you whelp," said the man in the chair.

"Shut up—ye," replied the sheriff, administering a stout cuff to the prisoner's ear. "Ye best hold yer tongue, man."

Just here Alma and John returned with the lantern. Under Elmer's directions they hung the sheet over one of the windows, and then the young man prepared his apparatus for a small trial of lantern projections. Mr. Denny sat in his chair silent and wondering. He knew not what to say or do, and watched these preparations with the utmost attention.

"Mr. Sheriff, if you please, you will stand near Mr. Belford, to prevent him from attempting mis-

chief when I darken the room. John, you may put
out all the candles save one."

Alma took her father's hand and kneeled upon
the floor beside him as if to aid and comfort him.

"Now, John, set that candle just outside the
door in the entry."

A sense of awe and fear fell on them all as the
room became dark, and none save the young son
of science dared breathe. Suddenly a round spot
of light fell on the sheet, and its glare illuminated
the room dimly.

"Before I show the will, Mr. Sheriff, I wish you
to see a photo that may be of use to you in that
little matter in the village of which you were speaking."

Two dusky figures slid over the disk of light.
They grew more and more distinct.

"It's Alice Green!"

A passion of weeping filled the room, and Elmer
opened the lantern, and the room became light.
Alma, with her head bent upon her father's knee,
was bathed in tears.

"Poor, poor lost Alice!"

"And the fellow with her? Who is he?" cried
the sheriff.

"That is Mr. Belford—Mr. Lawrence Belford,"
said Elmer with cool confidence. "That picture
was taken through a telescope from my room on
the morning of the 13th."

"The 13th! Why, man, that was the day she was missed."

"Yes. Mr. Belford was with her that day, and perhaps he can explain her disappearance."

The prisoner groaned in abject terror and misery. He saw it all now. His dream pictures were explained. His defeat and detection were accomplished through the young man's science. That he should have been overthrown by such simple means filled him with mortification and anger.

"You shall have the picture, Mr. Sheriff.. You may need it at the trial. And now for the will."

The room became again dark, and the figures on the wall stood out sharp and distinct on the sheet. Then the picture faded away, and in its place appeared writing—letters in white upon black ground:

"SALMON FALLS, June 1, 1869.

"I, Edward Denny, do hereby leave and bequeath to my son, John Denny, all of my property, both real and personal. All other wills I have made are hereby annulled. My near death prevents a more formal will.

"EDWARD DENNY.

"Witness:

"JOHN MAXWELL, M.D."

"My father's will."

There was a heavy fall, and Elmer opened his lantern quickly. It was too much for the old man. He had fallen upon the floor insensible.

"A light, John, quick."

They lifted him tenderly, and with Alma's help the old sheriff and the serving man took him away to his room.

The moment the two men were alone, the prisoner in the chair broke out in a torrent of curses and threats. The young man quietly took up his revolver, and said sternly:

"Lawrence Belford, hold your peace. Your threats are idle. You insulted me outrageously the day I came here. I bear you no malice, but when you attempted your infamous plan to capture my cousin and to ruin her father, I sprang to their rescue with such skill as I could command. We shall not pursue you with undue rigor, but with perfect justice."

"Oh, Mr. Franklin, have mercy upon me! Let me go! Let me escape before they return. I will go away—far away! Save me, save me, sir! I never harmed you. Have mercy upon me!"

"Had you shown mercy perhaps I might now. No, sir; justice before mercy. Hark— the officer comes."

They unfastened the ropes about Belford, and released the wires, and in silence he went away into the night in the hands of his grisly Nemesis.

The young man flung himself upon the lounge in the library, and in a moment was fast asleep.

The red gold of the coming day crept up the eastern sky. The storm became· beautiful in its fleecy rains in the far south. As the stars paled, the sweet breath of the cool west wind sprang up, shaking the raindrops in showers from the trees. The birds sang and the day came on apace.

To one who watched it seemed the coming of a fairer day than had ever shone upon her life. The vanished storm, the fresh aspect of nature moved her to tears of happiness. Long had she watched the stars. They were the first signs of light and comfc ᷄ she had discovered, and now they paled before the sun. Thus she sat by the open window in the library and watched with a prayer in her heart.

She looked at the mantel clock. Half past four. In half an hour the house would be stirring. All was now safe. She could return to her room. She rose and approached the sleeper on the lounge. He slept peacefully, as if the events of the night disturbed him not.

He smiled in his dreams, and murmured a name indistinctly. She drew back hastily and put her hand over her mouth, while a bright blush mounted to her face. Just here, through the sweet, still air of the morning, came the sound of the village· bell. Tears gathered in her eyes and fell unheeded upon her hands, clasped before her.

" Poor—lost—Alice—nineteen—just my age."

" Alma."

She turned toward the sleeper with a startled cry. He was awake and sitting up.

" What bell is that ? "

" It is tolling. They have found her."

" Yes, it is a sad story. Alma ! "

She advanced toward him. He noticed her tears and the morning robe in which she was dressed.

" What is it, Elmer ? Do you fell better ? "

" Yes. It was a sorry night for us."

" But the storm has cleared away."

He did not seem to heed what she said.

"How long have you been up ? "

" Since it happened. After I saw father upstairs I came down and found you here asleep. And, Elmer—forgive me—it was wrong, but I did not mean to stay here so long."

" Alma ! "

" You will pardon me ? "

" Oh ! Pardon you—pardon you—why should I ? I dreamed the angels watched me."

" I was anxious, and we owe you so much. We can never reward you—never ! "

" Reward, Alma ! I want none—save——"

" Save what ? "

He opened his arms wide. A new and beautiful light came into her eyes.

" Can there be greater reward than love ? "

" No. Love is the best reward—and it is yours."

LOVE AND A LANTERN.

BARSTOW'S SIDING is a small station on the G. S. and Western Railway, and located out on the prairie at the edge of a bit of scrubby woods. The little village of Barstow is about a mile from the station, and to reach it one has to take a rough road through the woods. The line at this point is perfectly straight, and reaches to the horizon in both directions. These facts are essential to a right understanding of the events that took place at the station one night about a year ago.

Old Sam Britton, station-master, sat by the stove in the middle of the switch-house idly looking at the dull red coals in the ugly stove. His daughter Mary, aged nineteen, sat by the little telegraph apparatus near the window that looked out down the line. By the aid of a lantern she was reading a stray newspaper, *The Iron Trade Review*—a strange paper for a girl to read, but it belonged to a dear friend, and some singular pictures had interested her greatly. She was doing more. She read and listened. Not a thing stirred in the dull, bare room save the restless sounder on her table. The incessant clatter of the machine fell on her ear, and yet she heard it not. Elm City was talking to Centreville, forty miles through the night, and every word was spelled on her sounder. Yet she heard it not, for her mind was alert to catch another sound. Her father had let fall the paper he was reading. He could not read, for a bitter disappointment kept his mind harassed and troubled. How long was this default of payment to the employés of the railway company to continue? The last month's wages had not been paid, and another month had nearly passed. The line needed repairing. There were two bad ties on this section, and one of the signals was broken. The track-men had complained that very day that new and better tools were needed, and that more ballast was wanting.

Suddenly, far away on the edge of the sea-like horizon, arose a star. The young girl's eyes were on the paper, and yet she saw its rising. She looked out the curtainless window and watched the star grow bright. It did not seem to rise, but to grow big with brightness. It is not for love to sit and gaze. It must act. She rose, and in silence went to one of the great iron switch-bars and stood with both hands clasped about the handle, and gazing down the line, where the star had become a flame.

Then came a far-away sound through the night.

Without hesitation she pulled the bar forward. Far down the track the switch moved in the dark, and a great green eye turned red. Up the line, in the opposite direction, another green star suddenly turned to a warning red.

Samson Gilder sat on his high seat with one hand on the throttle-valve, gazing steadily ahead. A constellation of green and yellow stars had sprung up on his horizon. Jack Cinder, his fireman, on the other side of the engine, had given voice to the monster as it panted along its iron way. Ah! one star had flashed red. The engineer blushed and smiled in the dark and pulled the throttle-valve. Then came a push and jar as the heavy freight-train rumbling behind pushed against the engine. The motive power had ceased, and the immense momentum of the train drove the idle engine swiftly forward. The whistle spoke to the men behind, and they gladly pulled at the brakes, and the train entered the siding. The head-light threw a lurid glare on the switch-house, and by the light Samson saw a young girl standing by the track. She was dressed for rough weather, and wore a red hood that was not lovely. Samson thought it was beautiful in the glow of the great lamp and against the winter night. It may have been the peculiar effect of the light. It may have been love, for love has finer eyes than unloving mortals.

They came into the switch-house together, she smiling and happy, he pleased and gratified, yet with a shade of care upon his face. In his hand he held a new tracklayer's bar, a bar such as may be used to draw spikes from ties.

He spoke to Sam Britton pleasantly about the weather, and then said, " There's a bar for the section-master. I bought it myself. The company seems to be too poor to give its men proper tools—"

" To say nothing of our wages," added the old man, roughly.

" Oh, father, why do you harp on that? The company has a great deal of property. It will surely pay us our dues."

The engineer placed the bar against the wall by the door, and then turned to Mary. She led him away to her little desk by the window, and there they sat down together. Presently Jack Cinder and one or two of the train men came and sat down by the dull red stove. The conversation among the men for the first few moments had a local flavor, and needs no mention. Then it branched to a more important theme—the over-due wages. Even the lovers discussed the matter, and after a few words they stopped abruptly. Tears brimmed the girl's eyes, and she turned away and gazed out the window at the glowing head-light.

Then one of the brakemen said : "And the president is racing round the country in a drawing-
room car. He's coming up the road to-night on a
special, and everything has to give way to his
train."

"I wish he might get tumbled into the ditch,"
said a deep voice that startled them all.

"Oh, Samson, how could you say that?"

"Because I'm mad. Here we can't—" He
stopped, and the girl blushed scarlet. "The president can make excursions over the line, and disarrange all the time-tables, and yet we are two
months waiting for our pay. I think—"

He stopped and looked toward the door ; a hideous creature, half man, half beast, stood unbidden
before them all. A tramp, foot-sore, homeless,
and hungry, he had found the door unlatched, and
had wandered in looking for shelter. The station-
master permitted the man to come in and stand
behind the stove to warm himself, for he was nigh
perishing with the cold, and then the conversation
lapsed into whispers.

Suddenly there came the sound of a. distant
whistle. The station-master looked at the switch
bars to see that the line was clear, and Samson
Gilder rose and said : "That's William's train. I'll
go out and wave him a friendly light as he passes."

The sound of the approaching freight-train came
nearer, and the engineer took the lantern from the

desk and went out. The others fell into silence as the rumbling train crept past the door. The young girl stared at the great head-light in sorrowful silence, thinking, wishing, and hoping.

Taking advantage of the noise, the tramp shuffled away toward the door. Just as he reached it he looked hastily round the room, and then slyly picked up the tracklayer's bar and disappeared. His presence had been a burden ; he had happily taken himself off, and they paid no heed to his departure. A moment after the door opened, and Samson Gilder entered. " The special is in sight, boys. We must be off."

The men reluctantly went out to their train, and the lovers met to part at the door. Her eyes were bright with ill-suppressed tears.

" It seems so long to wait—and all for a little money."

. " I know it, dear ; yet, when the company do pay up, we shall have all the more."

Nearer and nearer came the great yellow star that had sprung up on the horizon. From far came the long, wailing sound of the express whistle. The lovers heard it, and held each a tighter clasp. The tracks before the door began to " sing." The monster came on in frightful fury. Sparks shot up in fountains from its stack. The ground quivered, the windows shook, with its tread.

Ah ! a despairing scream from the whistle.

An earthquake.

Some one rushed past the girl. She clasped the door for support, not knowing what had happened. She looked out into the night, stunned and terrified.

There was nothing—nothing, save a vast cloud of dust, white and ghostly in the night. Ah! a gleam, a flare of light. It shone through the curtain of dust as it drifted away before the wind. There were hurrying footsteps, shouts, cries for help, and groans. The dust disappeared, and the end of an overturned car stood out in the bright light. The flames shot up higher. The wreck grew in horrid proportions. Ah! it was on fire.

It is a peculiar feature of American life that new and unexpected circumstances are always met and controlled by a spirit of organization that creates out of the men and materials at hand the mastery of events. In half an hour after the first crash, as the train left the metals, the frightened passengers were comfortably housed in the empty cars of the freight-train. A car-load of lumber had been despoiled to make seats for the whole and beds for the injured. The freight-engine on the siding was used to drag the wreck away from the up line, and its tank water and steam had been used to put out the fire. In an hour the freight-engine, in charge of the express people, started away with its dreary load, the well in the forward cars, the injured, on beds of hay robbed from the freight, in the next cars, the dead behind.

Darkness and silence fell on the lonely way-station, and save where the black wreck lifted its mangled bones against the sky, there was nothing to mark the disaster except the pale faces of the men who gathered round the stove in the switch-house. For a long time nothing was said. There are times when speaking seems impertinent. Events become too big for words. Then one of the men spoke and said,

"They did say it were the president who were killed in the forward sleeper."

Mary Britton glanced at Samson Gilder. He was silent and self-absorbed, and his face gave no indication that he heeded this remark. At that moment the door opened and Jack Cinder came in, bringing in his hand a new track-layer's bar. He brought it to the light and held it before them all.

"Do you see that, boys? I found it under the smashed sleeper. It's a new bar, and—" The men looked at the bar for a moment in apparent indifference, and said nothing. The keener feminine mind sprang to intuitive conclusions. Her thoughts leaped from a terror to a defense.

"It was the tramp. He stole the bar and wrecked the train."

"Mebbe he did, and mebbe he didn't. This I do know : Samson Gilder was a-wishing the president into the ditch. This is his bar, and he was out on the line just before it happened."

The coroner's jury called to consider the death of Thomas Starmore and others, killed at Barstow's Siding on the night of the 25th of February, met at the switch-house and heard the evidence of the persons who were known to have been present at the time of the disaster. Even the tramp had been captured. He was seen prowling in the woods near the line, and had been caught by the section master and his men. Every one at once said, "The tramp did it." But the tramp had in his hand another bar just like the bar found under the train. He admitted having stolen the bar. He had seen the disaster from the woods, and had then run away lest he be caught. After some time he had come back to find the bar he had dropped in the woods in his flight. He had the bar with him when caught. He could prove all this, because the bar was rusty from lying in the snow.

The reporters of the Centreville papers who were present called Mary Britton to the telegraph that a message might be dispatched. One of them placed a paper before her: "A tramp has been found who admits having stolen a bar, but it is plain that he did not use it. All the evidence goes to show that the engineer wrecked the train out of spite against the president."

10

These words Mary Britton sent off by wire to the whole United States, while her lover sat near, already in the shadow of advancing calamity. The operators who read off these words in distant cities heard every word distinctly, little knowing the terrible trial under which they were dispatched. Never in after-life did she forget that message.

"Gentleman," said the coroner, "this case seems to warrant me in referring the whole matter to the Grand Jury for further examination."

Weeks passed, and then the trial came on at the court-house at Centreville. Samson Gilder had been committed to answer a charge of wilfully wrecking a railroad train.

Mary Britton lived years in these few weeks. She could not believe Samson had committed so great a wrong. Yet every thing was against him. Track-layers' bars were abundant enough. He could easily have found one about the place, and with it have drawn the spikes from a rail. Her mind went backward and forward over all this a hundred times in search of something to prove him innocent. She still attended to her duties at the station, daily sending and receiving messages. One morning, as she sat thinking bitterly of the sorrow that had invaded her life, her eyes fell on an old newspaper fallen under her desk. She picked it up and opened it. *The Iron Trade Review.* She eagerly turned to the second page.

Ah! why had she forgotten these pictures?
Strange black figures, etchings of iron, nature-
printed. Given this slight clew, her mind leaped
to a brave resolve. She would bring science to
love's rescue. How, she could not tell. She had
a vague idea of what might be done, and, asking
her father to attend to the telegraph, she ran
hastily out on the line and down the road toward
the village. Stopping at a certain house, she
found a young girl who was a good operator, and
at once hired her to take her place at the station.

Before night she had taken every dollar she had
in the world from the savings-bank, and was on her
way to the city. The moving cars seemed to drag
too slowly. Why had she lingered so long idle,
and Samson in danger?

The day of the trial came on. At the trial all
the testimony that we already know, and much
more of less importance, had been offered by the
prosecution. The defense set up the previous
good character of the prisoner, and that seemed
about all that could be said.

Mary Britton had given her testimony early in
the trial, and that seemed to be all that she could
do. She had more to say, but was not yet ready
to speak. All the morning she had sat in the
crowded court-room, watching the clock, and waiting and looking for some one, a strong and brave
helper, to come to her assistance. At the last mo-

ment she spoke to the counsel, and asked for a slight delay. There might be yet other witnesses. The defense began to talk against time, and a messenger was sent to hasten the lagging aid.

The knight arrived. A pale, thin-faced young man in glasses appeared, and demanded to give his testimony. Behind him came a marvellous array—men with strange tools, lanterns of singular construction, bars and rods of iron, and a number of gentlemen who seemed to be prosperous merchants and manufacturers. There came also an old German Jew and a farmer from Barstow's. The young man spoke to Mary Britton with the utmost deference, and she consulted with him for a moment, and then presented him to Samson's counsel.

There was a slight murmur of surprise at this demonstration, and then Samuel Mayer was duly sworn. He testified that he was an expert in metals. He had examined the bar found under the wrecked car, and was prepared to prove that Samson Gilder coûld not have used it in wrecking the train. With the permission of the Court he would like to have the room darkened, that with the aid of a lantern he might project some nature-printed pictures of the iron used in making the bar.

The prosecution objected. What scientific jugglery was this ? The old lantern dodge familiar in cases of forgery. The Court overruled the objection, and the young man produced some pieces of cloth, which his assistants quickly spread over the windows, till the room became quite dark. A gas jet was lighted, and in the dim light other men set up a screen and lime-light lantern as for lantern projections. In a wonderfully short time there appeared on the white screen a strange figure—a cloud or blotch of blackness.

Samuel Mayer then testified that at the request of Miss Britton he had planed one side of each of the two bars till a smooth surface had been obtained. A portion of this surface on each bar had then been etched with acid, and from this etching had been obtained nature-printed copies or prints in ink. This well-known method of etching gave prints showing the disposition of the particles of the metal, and serving to show its quality. These etchings and a vast number of others taken from other bars and rods made by the different iron-makers of the country had been photographed for lantern projection, and, with the permission of the Court, some of these would be exhibited to the jury. The projection now on the screen was from the bar purchased by Gilder and stolen by the tramp.

Every eye was fixed on the singular picture on the screen, and a murmur of applause filled the room. Suddenly the picture was removed, and another took its place. It did not require much attention to show that this represented an entirely different kind of metal.

" This, gentlemen," said the young man, " is a nature-printed etching from the iron bar found under the car. I have compared these two etchings with a great number of etchings obtained in the same way from bars made by all the iron-men in the country, and I find this one corresponds exactly with etchings of the Moorlow Iron Company's metal. My assistant will place a sample of the company's iron beside this."

At once another picture sprang up beside the one on the screen. The two were exactly alike.

Another witness took the stand—the president of the Moorlow Iron Company. He testified to the facts of the experiments and to the results that had been obtained. ·

Another witness was called—the buyer of the railroad company. He testified that the company had never used the Moorlow Company's iron. The bar Gilder had bought had been obtained of Ross, Duncan & Co., of Pittsburg, from whom the railroad obtained all its tools.

Another etching was projected; then another appeared by its side. The two were exactly alike.

" The picture on the right," said Mayer, " is Ross, Duncan & Co.'s iron. That on the left is the etching shown first, and obtained from the bar purchased by Gilder."

The judge rapped smartly on his desk. This applause could not be permitted again. The daylight was re-admitted, and the pictures faded away. Photographs of the etching were handed to the jurors, and the various samples of iron from which the etching had been obtained were exhibited.

Samson Gilder sat with face averted. How could he deserve such love? It was too divine a gift. Why had he not known of her surpassing love for him, her mastery of mind and will that could accomplish such results, and all for him? He did not deserve so great a blessing.

Some one else was testifying. A farmer living at Barstow had passed a man on the road, just before the accident, who muttered to himself, " I'll have my revenge, whoever may suffer."

Abraham Samuels testified that he had bought the old junk and refuse from the wreck, and had found a coat much torn, and probably belonging to a passenger. In the coat was part of a letter— a threatening letter addressed to " John Morley."

" He was killed in the wreck," said Mary Britton, with sudden eagerness.

" Silence ! Let the witness proceed."

This letter threatened John Morley with death for some past injury, and warned of some impending disaster. It was signed, " Fred Smythe."

There was a sudden movement at the rear of the court, and every one turned to see what it meant.

A man was pushed roughly out of the seats, as if eager to escape.

"Sixty!" cried the farmer from Barstow; "that's the feller I saw just afore the smash."

"It was a remarkable case," said the judge to his colleague, after the trial. "The woman must have been a person of extraordinary mind, to have planned the scheme, and to have won all those scientific people over to her side. I understand she had not a cent in the world, and could pay them nothing. Women will do anything for love."

PUT YOURSELF IN HER PLACE.

THE long summer day had crept slowly away, and it was nearly five o'clock. The hours at the railway station were marked as by some gigantic clock that told the laggard minutes by screaming whistle and clanging bell. The 4.30 accommodation had gone east, the western express, due there at 4.55, had thundered through the village, gone on over the great viaduct, and disappeared round the vast curve beyond.

So one counted the hours by the trains, Lydia by name, a girl of the best New England type, quiet, and yet with an immense capacity for doing and daring should love and the occasion demand. The local freight would come next and then,—then she would see *him* again. She laid aside her work, put some split-zephyr vanity upon her head and went out toward the railroad. As she approached the station she saw her brother, the station-master, opening the little freight-house on the farther side of the track. By this she knew that the local freight would stop this time. Her heart beat the faster and she quickened her step.

10*

On reaching the passenger station where the village street crossed the railway, she looked up and down the line and then crossed over and turned to the left and walked beside the track toward the freight-house.

To understand all that took place on this occasion, and to fully appreciate her consummate skill in controlling the events so quickly to crowd upon her, we must study the construction of the road at this point. The Main Line for more than a mile to the right, or toward the east, was perfectly straight and comparatively level. To the left, or the west, it crossed a deep valley by a lofty stone viaduct, and beyond the valley it curved toward the north and mounted the hill by a long grade. Just east of the passenger station a branch road entered the Main Line and there was, as might be supposed, a cross-over switch. Beyond the passenger station, on the west, was a short siding ending in a small freight-house, and directly opposite was another siding with a freight-shed and coal-yard. At this point there was also another cross-over switch.

Lydia walked on past the freight-house, and, crossing the side track, found a large flat rock beside the way, and there, under the shade of an ancient apple tree, she sat down to wait till her lover should come.

He comes! She heard the three long whistles

sounding far down the line, and a bright blush mounted to her face. The train would stop. That was the signal for the station-master. Her brother came out of the freight-house, spoke pleasantly to her, and then walked on toward the switch at the head of the siding.

Suddenly the Main Line track before her began to sing in sharp metallic murmurs. The train had entered that section of the road and *he* was near. Then there came the sound of escaping steam. The engine was slowing down and the steam, no longer employed, was bursting with a loud roar from the safety valve as if impatient of delay.

With a jar that shook the ground the immense freight-engine rolled past her, and the engineer, leaning out of his window, nodded to her as he slid past. Then the cars in long procession came into sight and moved past with slowly decreasing speed. Four brakemen busy at the brakes went past and still he came not. At last the rear car appeared, and a young man swung himself down from the iron ladder on the car and sprang to the ground at her feet.

A sooty man, clad in blue canvas now black with smoke and dust. Only a brakeman ! No ; a trifle better—the conductor of the freight train. A year ago he had been glad to take the place of a brakeman, and already he had been promoted. Love did it. He had met and loved Lydia in the days

of his foolish idleness, and she had insisted that he
do some manly work or she could not—yes, she
could and did love him ; but he must show himself
worthy her love.   Already he had advanced, and
she was well pleased with his progress, and they
had become engaged.

A grimy, dusty man in unlovely garments ; but,
in her eyes, he was a man made for better things.
As he stood beside her one could see in his clear
eyes and sensible face that he had good stuff in him
and was worthy of her love.

It becomes us not to linger while they talk
quietly together beside the track.   The train
moved slower and slower till, finally, it stopped
with the last car just beyond the switch.   The iron
horse was moved on, the station-master signalled
with his arms in a curious fashion, and each of the
four brakemen repeated the motion in turn.   White
puffs of steam rose high in the air from the farther
end of the train.   A curious rattling sound spread
through the train, and the last car backed down,
turned aside, and entered the siding.   The station-
master left the switch and came hastily toward the
lovers.

" Good day, Alfred.   Light freight to-day, only
one car—by the way, the brake chain is broken,
and you had better drop the car at the repair
shops.   The freight can _be thrown out without
leaving the car."

So saying, the station-master went on into the freight house followed by the rattling and rumbling cars. They gradually lost their speed and then came to a stop with the end of the train lost in the dark cavern of the freight house. There was a shout from the building, and then one of the brakemen began to move his arms as a signal to go on. Again the white puffs of steam shot up in the distance and with a jar and quiver the train started again.

Car after car rolled past them. There were hurried whispers, a warm hand-shake and perhaps a kiss, and then the young man swung forward grasped the ladder on the last car, climbed quickly to the top and sat down. She stood gazing after him as he was drawn away from her, and smiled and waved farewell to him with her handkerchief.

"Here, Lydia, you must help me."

It was her brother who stood beside her with a bunch of keys in his hand.

"The passenger train follows this at once and I must go to the station. Will you please close the switch after them?"

She took the keys mechanically, and then turned again to gaze after her lover seated on the last car of the retreating train. It had passed out of the switch and was crossing the great viaduct and moving more and more swiftly away.

To close and lock the switch was neither difficult

nor dangerous, and she quietly walked on toward the end of the siding till she came to the switch-post. Here she leaned against the wooden frame for a little space, shading her eyes from the sun with her hand and watching the train. It had run around the valley and was turning into the great curve that crept upward in a long grade over the hill beyond.

It was now a mile away and she could no longer distinguish any one on the cars. She turned slowly away, seized the iron bar of the switch and easily threw it over into place so as to leave the Main Line open for the next train.

She looked back down the road and saw that the passenger train had entered the line from the branch and was just pulling up at the station to discharge passengers. It may seem surprising that a passenger train should be allowed to follow a freight train so closely.

Bad engineering as this arrangement was, it was not so serious as it seemed, for this passenger train did not follow the freight except for three miles, when it reached the end of its trip and was turned off upon a siding.

She turned once more to look after the retreating freight train. It was in full view climbing the grade on the great curve.

Suddenly she put up both hands to shade her eyes, and leaned forward on the switch frame.

What had happened? Two tiny puffs of steam rose from the engine. It was the signal to stop.

Ah! the train has parted! Faint and far away came the short, sharp danger whistle. A single car had broken loose from the train, and had been left behind. It was standing alone on the track.

No. It was moving backward. It was beginning to roll down the grade. It was moving faster and faster. There was a man upon it—her lover.

Involuntarily she spread out her arms and let them fall to her side three or four times in succession—the signal to put on the brakes.

"How foolish! He cannot see me, and—" She leaned against the switch-frame and shook with fear and agony.

The brake was broken.

Swift and swifter rolled the disabled car. It was coming down the track gaining speed at every rod.

She sprang to the middle of the track and tried to shout to the engineer of the train at the station. She made the motions to back down out of danger. Her tongue clove to the roof of her mouth and her cry became an inarticulate moan.

Onward came the car. She could see her lover upon it frantically waving his arms from right to left. What did it mean? Her brain seemed to be on fire. She could do nothing, but gaze on the advancing car in dumb horror.

Ah! The passengers! Could she not save them?

With a violent wrench she opened the switch again and stood holding the bar in both hands. Better so,—better one life lost than a dozen. Her feet seemed bolted to the ground. She must stay and see him killed, and by her own hand.

The rails began to murmur with the tread of the advancing car now rushing furiously onward to destruction.

Ah! why had she not thought of it before?

The cross-over switch! Could she reach it in time she might save him. She snatched the key from the switch and ran with frantic speed up the line. She never knew how she opened that switch.

With moans and cries she threw herself across the line and began to run down the other side. Could she reach that switch before the car? Its roaring rang in her ears. Panting, with almost bursting bosom she reached the switch, opened it and stood clinging to it as the car came thundering over the viaduct.

She looked up at her lover upon the car. He had seen and understood the change in the switches. His car, helpless though it was, would cross over to the down track and roll harmlessly along the level line till its force was spent. He was saved, and by her ready wit and skill. The passengers in the train were also saved.

She had saved him. Love had been her inspiration.

Great Heavens! what's that? The express! The down express was coming!

All was in vain. He was lost. She saw him throw up his arms in despair. The very plan she had devised to save him would be his destruction. Better far to have thrown him off upon the siding as she had intended. Now he would meet a more dreadful death and the destruction would include scores of lives instead of a dozen.

All this flashed through her mind like as lightning. She felt her knees give way beneath her and she clung to the switch in despair. She shut her eyes to hide the coming disaster.

Hark! The whistle of the express. They had seen the imminent collision and were doing their best to avert it.

She, too, must do something. With a bound she sprang to the next switch, tore it open and stood panting and moaning beside it with the bar in her hand. She must save the train even if she buried her lover under the splintered wreck of the car.

Onward came the car, thundering over the viaduct and just ahead of the train. It turned quickly at the switch, crossed over and shot past her into the siding. He had one look at her upturned face. It was full of love and helpless misery. She was sending him to certain destruction—to save the express train.

The instant the car passed she closed the switch and sprang back again to the other switch and closed it just in time to see the express train sweep past in safety.

In an instant the helpless car ran into the freight-house with an awful splintering crash. The express pulled up opposite the station and in a moment a crowd of people ran shouting and frantic up the line. Some of them had seen the whole performance and knew what it meant, but for the majority of them it was a tragic mystery.

They found Lydia upon the ground by the switch, and with the keys still clutched in her hand. What had she done? What had happened to her?

She could not answer. Nature had mercifully taken away her senses. They took her up tenderly and carried her to the station and laid her upon a seat in the waiting-room. The passengers of the two trains crowded the room and offered every aid, for in some vague manner they began to understand that she was the creditor to the value of all their lives. She had paid for their safety with costly sacrifice.

The freight train backed down to the cross-over switch and the engineers of the three trains met and began to examine the positions of the switches. A number of men also came from the express train, and among them was one who seemed in authority. He, too, examined the line carefully, and the engineers explained the matter to him, and listened to his remarks with becoming deference.

The little room in the station was packed with people, idlers and others, and they could with difficulty bring *him* in.

" No," said one of the ladies who were trying to restore the girl. " It may be too great a shock for her. She must not see him yet."

" Make way there, gentlemen. The superintendent of the road is here."

The crowd moved slightly, and the superintendent advanced into the room. He took off his hat and spoke quietly to the people near, and then he stooped over the unconscious girl and softly kissed her like as a father.

" She saved all our lives and I fear she thinks she paid dearly for them."

Suddenly she opened her eyes and sat up bewildered.

" Where is he ? Is he much hurt ? Oh ! Perhaps he is ——"

" Let me alone, I tell you," cried a big, bold voice in the crowd, " I must go to her."

He escaped from those who would detain him and in a moment was beside her.

Some of the people laughed in foolish joy, others cried. The more delicate and sensible were silent, for the meeting was not for words or descrip·tion.

After a slight pause the superintendent said to the young man :

" I congratulate you, sir.   You were on the car ? "

" Yes, sir.   I was on the car and I saved myself at the last moment by jumping off.   I landed on a pile of fine coal and got a rough tumble—and that was all.   The car is a heap of splinters."

Then the superintendent called the young man nearer to him and spoke to him privately, and presently they both shook hands as if greatly pleased over something.   The young man sat down beside the girl and whispered in her ear.

" I've got the place, Lydia.   We're all right now."

Then the bells rang, and the people began to disperse toward their trains.   As they departed, a small creature—probably a stockholder—objected to the proceedings and remarked to the superintendent that " it was not best to give fat offices to brakemen for doing nothing."

" Precisely," said the superintendent.   " But the woman did something, and if you wish to know the full measure of her splendid deed, go put yourself in her place."

THE WRECK OF THE PIONEER.

RALPH KEYSTONE was one of those men who combine a talent for practical things with an active imagination. He was, at the same time, a most unpractical man in affairs of business. Like all imaginative men, he early found a woman whom he could clothe in ideal charms, and then fell in love with her. Jane Besant was the only daughter of Farmer Besant, who owned and operated an immense wheat farm not far from the village of Muskalontic. To Farmer Besant went Ralph in the first flush of his love for Jane.

" You wish to marry Jane ? "

The young man replied, " Not immediately,". for just at the time he was out of employment.

" That's just it, Keystone," said the farmer ; " you are out of work for the fourth time since you came from the East. How can you marry on so uncertain a prospect ? You are too unstable ; you do not stick to anything."

Ralph admitted he had been unfortunate in his ventures ; but he still had a little money left, and

he would now go into some manufacturing business.

"Manufacturing, indeed! There's nothing but
farms within fifty miles. Wheat is the only thing
that pays here, unless it be lumber, and there isn't
a saw-mill within a hundred miles."

"Then I might start one," said Ralph, catching
at this straw, for he felt himself sinking. He could
make no headway against this hard, practical man,
who knew nothing beyond wheat.

"Start a saw-mill! Where's your power?
And, if you had it, how could you compete with
the mills up the river? Look here, Ralph, I don't
want to be hard on you. I see you love Jane, and
Jane loves you—at least she seems to think so."

"That's the truth," said Ralph. "We love each
other dearly."

"Now I'll make a bargain with you. If you
will go into some business, and make it a success,
you shall have Jane—that is, if she wants you."

"Thank you, sir," said the young man. "I'll
start the saw-mill at once."

The road to the village followed the river for
some distance through Farmer Besant's land, and
then turned east through the woods toward the
village. Ralph walked along in a dazed fashion,
mentally numb with his refusal, his body walking
automatically, just as it will when the mind is ab-
sorbed in contemplation. At the turn of the road

his feet took the right direction for home, but after going a few steps he stopped abruptly, and turned back to the river.   The Muskalontic is a wide, shallow stream, winding sluggishly through the country, its banks being hereabouts heavily fringed with woods.

The young man left the road and followed the shore down stream, walking quickly, as if looking for something.   Like all imaginative people, he had been given to wandering about the country, and was familiar with the land for miles around Muskalontic.   He remembered having seen falling into the river, between two low hills, a slender brook, half lost in the woods.

Just as he had supposed.   It was a living stream, still running, though it was August.   He looked at the tiny run for a moment, and then started briskly up its winding channel, carefully noting the slope and character of the ground.   After walking a short distance he found the little valley narrowed, and then spread out into a slough, a marsh, where the stream was lost in pools and sedges.

Like a prospector searching for precious metals when he finds a vein, he threw up his hat with a cheer.

" I've won her !   I fancy the old gentleman will let us marry now."

Had Farmer Besant been within hearing, he

would have smiled at this counting of unhatched chickens. Your imaginative man sees power in a brook. With power to let or sell, a man may buy fortune. Just then there came through the woods the sound of a passing steamer on the river, and the young man smiled.

" I'll beat those fellows yet. They take all this trade up the river, and leave this farming region to stagnate. We must have manufactories here, and they shall begin with a saw-mill."

So it is the imaginative man finds wealth in the ground, and, if he be of the right stamp, he proceeds to realize his dreams. Keystone sat up all night over his drawing-paper and pencils. Two days after saw three woodmen felling trees by the little brook. The land belonged to Farmer Besant, and he had consented that a dam should be erected thereon. If Keystone was fool enough to sink his money in improving the bit of water-power he thought he had found, he was at liberty to do so, provided he gave half the work when finished to the land-owner, with half the lumber cut on the land. If he failed, then all the lumber was to remain on the land. Pretty hard terms, but Ralph accepted them on the spot.

Axe in hand he headed the woodmen, directing the fall of each tree, so as to save labor in hauling the logs. When about a hundred trees were down, he organized his force into choppers, and began to get out logs of every size. A pair of oxen were hired, and things began to assume shape. Heavy logs laid end to end in a double row stretched across the little valley, and marked the foundation of the dam. Stout stakes were driven on the lower side, and shorter logs laid up stream, with the ends resting on the heavy timbers, raised the dam about one foot. The news quickly spread through the country round about. Young Keystone had found water-power—in other words, wealth—in the little brook. Within three weeks the dam had been raised three feet, and the water began to back up behind it, spreading out over the marsh in a slowly widening pond. Then the people began to laugh. Keystone was a fool, after all. What could he do with only three feet fall of water?

Jane Besant heard of all this with mingled pride and hope. She wandered down to look at the work one Sunday afternoon. She went alone, not wishing to be seen showing too much interest in the affair. As she walked through the woods she came suddenly upon the clearing, and saw the sheet of water sparkling and blue in the bright sunshine. Her eyes shone with pleasure at the beauty of the sight. He had made this, his talents had created the pretty lake, and, better still, had won power from the idle brook.

She walked down to the dam, and paused to admire the work. Entirely unfamiliar with such

11

structures, it seemed quite wonderful. The great logs were dripping with water, here and there tiny fountains showed how the pent-up water was trying to escape, and in one place it poured over in a murmuring cascade.

"Oh! I knew he had genius. He has more talent than any man in the place."

Suddenly she was startled by a laugh, and turning she found her father near.

"It does look as if he had talent, Jane; but the fact is, he is a fool. It's a very pretty piece of work, and it must have cost a good bit of money; but I'm told by them that knows, it won't work. The fall is too low, and the whole thing is a failure."

"I don't know anything about such matters, father"—tears of mortification and disappointment filled her eyes—"but Ralph is not a fool." ·

"Well, maybe he isn't. I'm only telling you what folks say."

"There's not a man in the township knows a thing about hydraulic engineering. It's a good science, for I've been reading about it."

"All right, Jane. Give him a chance. Let's see how he pulls through. I don't really call him a fool, though he's mighty green at times."

The next day a small party of laborers appeared in the woods, and by night they had dug a long ditch or canal from the river up the bed of the

brook. Two days after, it reached the foot of the
dam, and brought the river water close up to the
logs. At the upper end it was five feet deep. Five
and three make eight. Eight feet fall in the clear.
Here's power in abundance. Thereupon the on-
lookers said the young man was a smart fellow, a
good engineer, etc., etc. Within a week the village carpenter had constructed a water-wheel from
Ralph's designs. Within two weeks saws and
gearing arrived, a shed was put up, and the saw-
mill was opened for business.

The first job was for a lot of two-inch plank for
Farmer Besant. He claimed that he was half
owner of the mill by their agreement, and would
only pay half the bill. Keystone took the job,
and soon had it finished, and even ran through a
lot of logs and piled up the planks on sale. Sundry small jobs came in, and it began to look as if
he had started a good business. One morning a
stranger arrived, and introduced himself as a lumber dealer from a town fifty miles down the river.
He was in search of a lot of small stuff, light scantling two inches wide and an inch and a half thick,
in lengths of twelve feet and upward. He wanted
a million feet, and he offered a good price, and
gave his name and references. The offer was
tempting, and Ralph took it, and agreed to have
the stuff ready in two weeks. Encouraged by his
success, he hired more help, and started on the new

order. In ten days he wrote to the party to say that the scantling was nearly all ready, and could be put on a raft and floated down the river. No reply came, and he wrote again, and in a few days received a notification of the failure of the lumber dealer, and an account of the winding up of his affairs.

Discouraged and sick at heart, he wandered down by the river and sat down on a fallen tree alone. Everything was lost. He could never marry Jane. A large part of his lumber had been cut up into a useless and unsalable shape, and he was in debt to his men. In foolishly trusting the word of a stranger he had made a wreck of everything. When the mind is ill at ease a trifling circumstance will often absorb the whole attention, and as he sat gloomily brooding over the ruin of hopes, he saw a steamboat rounding the bend of the river about a mile up stream. She was steering dangerously near a half-sunken island in the middle of the river. He watched her with a vague curiosity as she came swiftly onward. Suddenly she turned, and with apparent purpose ran directly across the upper end of the island, struck and grounded. He could see the wheels reversed, and in a moment after saw the wildest confusion among the passengers on board. Springing up, he ran at full speed along the bank till he came opposite the stranded boat.

It was a freight and passenger steamer—the Pioneer by name. She blew her whistle loudly, and a moment after he saw a boat lowered. For an instant there was some confusion on the steamer, as if the people were demoralized, but a tall fellow interfered, and order was restored. The boat came slowly ashore, and by the time it had reached the bank all his mill-hands and several farming people had arrived in an excited crowd on the bank. In the boat came the captain of the steamer. As he sprang ashore he said to Ralph :

" Are there any boats or barges about here ? "

" Nothing but a punt or two. Can't you bring your passengers ashore in your own boats ? "

" Bother the passengers ! I can land them easy enough. It's the cargo. The steamer will never come off. The tiller rope broke, and she ran nose on at full speed. The old Pioneer has laid down her bones forever. Poor old tub ! I pity her."

The speech created the greatest excitement among the bystanders. The rural mind saw visions of salvage—perhaps plunder—in the wrecked steamer, and they were ready of one accord to go off to her in any manner of boat that could be made to float. Just then the captain dropped from his pocket, as if by accident, a revolver, and picking it up, he said, " There's to be no foolin' round the old Pioneer. I'm captain and owner, and I mean to stand by her till the last scrap of old iron is shipped down river."

"I'll take your cargo ashore, or down stream to any point you say, in three days, for five hundred dollars."

"Oh, you've a barge or two. Why didn't you say so? I'll hire 'em of you."

"I have no barge, but I'll make one in twenty-four hours—for cash. I have a saw-mill just back of here."

"I say, boss, want any help?"

Here was honest business, and they were as ready to take advantage of it as they were to plunder the helpless steamer.

"I'll give you five hundred dollars if you'll put the cargo on a flat within three days. I can't get a steamer up here in less than two days, and it will cost almost as much, though I don't see how you're going to make a flat in that time."

"That's my look out. I'll have a barge 'long-side before to-morrow night."

"It will take two barges. Heavy cargo this trip."

"If I leave a single barrel behind, I'll forfeit a hundred dollars. You can take the passengers to the village. Some of the folks will give them lodgings till the boats come up on Monday."

The captain agreed to the bargain, and put off to bring his passengers ashore.

"Johnson," said Ralph to one of the young men, "go to the painter's, and tell him to send me three men and a lot of white-lead paint. Then get two kegs of sixpenny nails and bring them to the mill. Take my horse. Pick up all the men you can find. I want all the carpenters in the place to work day and night on a good job."

Ten minutes later a dozen men, with carpenters' tools, stood ready in the mill-yard waiting for orders.

" I was born next door to a Massachusetts ship-yard," said Ralph, "and I know something about boat-building. I am going to make a barge big enough for a steamboat. Let every man do exactly as I tell him, and we will have her launched before to-morrow night. Every man shall have double pay while at work on the boat."

The men gave a cheer, and said they were ready for anything. It seemed as if it might be true, for in a moment after they were carrying long two-inch planks down to the river-bank. Here a space was cleared next the water, and four lines of timber "ways," or slides, were laid down heading into the water, securely fastened together, and then liberally spread with grease and oil. Then, under Ralph's directions, two-inch planks were laid side by side on the ways till a platform was made one hundred and eighty feet long and about twenty feet wide in the centre. More men began to arrive, and every one who could drive nails was promptly engaged, and within an hour forty men were at work on the new boat.

With chalk and line Ralph struck a line through the centre of the platform, and from this struck out a curved line on each side, and then bade the men saw off the planks to the curved line. This gave a long slender platform, ten feet wide at the upper end, or stern, twenty feet wide near the centre, and running off to a long, slender point at the lower end, or bows, of the future boat. Then upon this platform was laid a rough coat of paint, a dozen men plying the brushes at once, and then came more planks laid lengthwise. The two platforms were cut to the same form, and were quickly spiked together.

The men suggested that such a long and slender raft would never hold together.

" Wait and see," said Ralph. " Now for the scantling we have been getting out at the mill. Bring it down by the cart-load. Now, men, have your bits ready for boring nail-holes in the stuff. Make the holes a foot apart the whole length of the strips."

In a moment or two several pieces of scantling were ready, and taking one in hand, Ralph laid it along the edge of the raft and nailed it down, then another, till a strip had been laid entirely round the raft. As the strips were long and flexible, they were easily bent to fit the curved lines of the platform. At the upper end the cross-pieces were nailed together, and at the bow end the strips were brought to a point, and fitted to an upright piece set up at the end of the platform. Then through the centre of the platform was laid another strip from end to end, while at intervals of about five feet cross-pieces were laid from side to side.

" Now, men, you see my idea. Lay strip over strip, and nail them firmly one to the other through the holes, till the sides are six feet high; break the joints of the strips and nail-holes; lay on the paint freely as you go, and we shall soon have a steamboat without ribs. The cross-pieces will brace her, and she'll carry a big cargo, even if she isn't very pretty."

The men, unaccustomed to marine architecture, greeted this novel system of boat-building with pleased surprise, and went to work with a will. More men arrived, and the clatter of twenty ham-mers going at once made the woods ring. The sun went down, and torches and bonfires were lighted. A boy was sent round for the men's sup-per that there might be no delay. The passengers of the wrecked steamer were bestowed in sundry farm-houses, Farmer Besant taking his share at two dollars each. The news of the boat-building spread quickly, and the people flocked down to the mill-yard to see the work, and with them came

11*

all the passengers. Among them came Farmer Besant and the captain of the Pioneer. The Farmer walked about the curious structure now rapidly rising, and seeing the enormous consumption of scantling, he remonstrated in no pleasant mood.

" What right have you to use up your customer's stuff in this way ? "

" He's failed," said Keystone, without stopping his work.

"How do you know? He may claim it, and you are spoiling thousands of feet of good stuff on a piece of folly."

" Don't know about that," said a big fellow near by. " It's about the smartest idee I ever seen. Guess you belong East, young man ? "

" Massachusetts. I've seen many a boat built without ribs, though none quite so big. She'll carry your cargo, captain."

" Oh, she will when she's decked. Them Massachusetts boys are powerful 'cute at things. I say, young feller, don't you want to sell her just as she stands ? "

" No. She is to be a steamboat."

Farmer Besant felt confirmed in his views of young Keystone. He was a born fool—come from the very home of lunatics and visionaries.

" I'll give you three hundred dollars for her just as she stands, and finish her myself."

" The Jane is not for sale."

"Jane for sale? Don't insult the girl, Mr. Ralph."

"A little more paint—lay it on thick!" Then he turned away to drive more nails.

Farmer Besant went home, intending to tell Jane of the insult she had received. He would never speak to Keystone again, neither should Jane. Luckily Jane had gone to bed when he returned, and knew nothing of the building of the boat.

Morning came and saw the sides of the boat well advanced. Some men left for home and rest, and others took their places. Even some of the passengers volunteered as painters and nail-drivers. There was no thought of the Sabbath. The excitement of the wreck, the arrival of so many strangers, and the boat-building brought everybody out of doors, and the yard was filled with people watching the progress of the work. During the night a steamboat passed up stream, but did not stop longer than to ask if help was needed. The Pioneer slowly broke in two, and the stern settled down in the water. She would never come off, and would be dismantled and broken up. The crew saved the cargo from damage by moving it to the forward part of the boat, that was so far uninjured. By nine o'clock there were three hundred people in the new ship-yard. Carriages began to arrive from far and near. Even the parson went down to "see the work of humanity," as he called it, and the church was closed for the day, for there was no congregation, the people, to the number of five hundred, had with one accord met to see the launching of the boat.

Among them came one with shining eyes and a rosy blush upon her face. The name of her lover was on every tongue. The marked approval of the captain of the steamer, and the enthusiasm of his engineer, won the confidence of the rural population. Keystone had always been considered an eccentric sort 'of fellow, but now, after all, there might be something in him. These things she heard and treasured in her heart. She kept out of sight in the crowd, but saw everything and heard everything with the greatest interest and pleasure. There was a man painting letters in blue on the stern of the new boat. He had made a J, an A, and an N, and was at work on another letter. Ah, JANE—her name! There was quite a company of people watching the man, and when the name was finished there was a little shout of approval.

"I allers said he was dreffle sweet on Squire Besant's darter."

"Sho! That's a pretty idee, anyway."

She blushed scarlet, and slipped away and went up to the deserted saw-mill, and sat down on a log by the little water-fall. Suddenly some one stood beside her.

"Oh, Jane! It's all over. I have failed, and to-morrow your father will take the mill. That lumber-dealer has failed, and that brings me down."

"Can't you sell the lumber?" said Jane, with ready common-sense.

"I have used a part of it in making the barge. If I get the money for saving the cargo, I shall have just enough to pay every bill, but with nothing left."

She stood up, and placing a hand on each shoulder, calmly kissed him.

"Thank you, love, for the compliment."

"I heard the engineer say the—the Jane would make a good freight steamer if she were engined."

"Did he? That's not a bad idea. I had thought she would make some kind of a craft. Oh! Perhaps I could buy the engines out of the steamer. They will sell them cheap."

"I thought you had failed and lost everything."

"No. I can't fail while I have you."

What further sentiment he would have indulged in cannot be known, for some one called them.

"She's 'bout ready to slide," said the big captain. Seeing Jane, he took off his hat and said, politely, "Will the young lady name the boat?"

"The boat is named the Jane Besant. Let me present my friend Miss Besant, captain."

"Glad to meet you, miss. I called my first boat the Nancy K., after my wife. It brings luck."

The built-up sides of the boat and the interior cross-work that braced her and held the hull together in every direction had been raised six feet high. Boards were laid down on top to form a deck, and she was ready to be put afloat. The captain and the engineer, Ralph, and about a dozen men armed with long poles mounted the deck. The word was given, the blocks were knocked away, and down she slid swiftly into the water amid the cheers of the people. She settled down in the water with a slight list to one side, and the rural population gave a little cry of alarm.

"The cargo will ballast her," said Ralph. "Get out your poles, men, and push her along the shore till we come to the steamer."

The Jane Besant was quickly brought round, and went up stream, followed by an enthusiastic multitude on the shore. Shortly after, the barge was secured alongside the wreck, and the men began to put the cargo on board. She did not leak a drop, and appeared to be as stiff and strong as the best ribbed boat afloat. She was very buoyant, and readily minded the rude rudder that had been hung at the stern.

"Come in my cabin—I guess it isn't wholly wrecked. Come, Bates, I want you too."

The young man followed the captain and his

engineer into the cabin and sat down, while the captain ordered some wine and a lunch. When the lunch came, the captain began to be expansive.

" She only wants a little more sheer, and a deck and house and engines. She'll not be a fast boat, but she'll go in shallower water than anything on the river. She'll be running regular trips when the big boats are laid up for low water. Tell you what I'll do, young man, I'll put engines in her and make her a stern-wheeler. Mebbe you can raise enough to put a house on her. I'll go halves with you in the business. We can haul her ashore and sheathe her bottom to make it smooth, and make a good thing of it. What d' you say? Is it a bargain?"

" It is Sunday, sir."

" Oh yes—forgot. Bargain not binding made to-day."

" It is the Sabbath."

" Yes, Sabbath. Wa'al, if you're of the same mind to-morrow, I'll repeat the offer. We can take the engines, Bates."

" Oh, certain, sir. That's all that's left good for anything on the Pioneer, 'cept it be parts o' the house."

" And the bedding, and furniture, and crockery, and so on."

" I shall be glad to consider your proposal, sir, to-morrow."

"Then it would be a bargain—if it wasn't Sunday. All right. We'll go ashore this evening and hear the parson."

Two months later the purser of the new freight and passenger boat Jane Besant opened the books of the boat for business. There was a line of passengers, headed by one of the boat's servants, already waiting at the ticket-office window.

"Mr. and Mrs. Ralph Keystone—oh yes—all right—free passes. Give them the bridal room, John; here's the key. Next!"